35 HIKING TRAILS
COLUMBIA RIVER GORGE

Second Edition

by
Don & Roberta Lowe

Frank
Amato

PORTLAND

AGENCY LISTINGS

Listed below are addresses and phone numbers for the government agencies having jurisdiction over the trails described in this guide. The relevant hike numbers are shown for each agency.

Beacon Rock State Park   1, 2
   Milepost 34.83L.
   State Road 14
   Skamania, Washington 98648
   (509) 427-8265

Wind River Ranger District   3
   Gifford Pinchot National Forest
   Carson, Washington 98610
   (509) 427-5645

Oregon State Parks   4, 16
   Rooster Rock State Park
   PO Box 100
   Corbett, Oregon 97019
   695-2261

Mt. Hood National Forest
   2955 NW Division Street
   Gresham, Oregon 97030
   666-0700

Columbia Gorge Ranger District   5, 6, 7, 8, 9, 10, 11, 12, 13, 14, 15,
   31520 SE Woodard Road   17, 18, 19, 20, 21, 22, 23, 24, 25,
   Troutdale, Oregon 97060   26, 27, 28, 29, 30, 31
   695-2276

Hood River Ranger District   32, 33, 34, 35
   6780 Highway 35
   Mt. Hood, Oregon 97041
   352-6002
   666-0701 (toll free from Portland)

Copyright © 1988
by Don & Roberta Lowe
ISBN 1-57188-010-0

INTRODUCTION

Of the 200 plus miles of trails in the Columbia River Gorge most are within an hour's drive of Portland and they provide some of the best hiking in the Northwest. This region of uncounted waterfalls, steep sided canyons and lush vegetation is indeed a remarkable place. Every portion of every route is scenic—no slogs through mediocre woods just to reach one viewpoint here. The hiking possibilities range from short, almost level strolls to complex, strenuous loops that can take one or more full days. And many of these superb routes are open almost all year, with each season having its special allure—the wildflowers of spring, the softness of summer, the varied hues of autumn and the starkness of winter.

Geomorphologically, the Columbia River Gorge extends east from Troutdale for some 55 miles to The Dalles, but, to most people, "the Gorge" means that stretch of rock walls and wooded slopes from Crown Point to Hood River. This impressive area is the result of successive layers of mudflows, basalt flows and other volcanic debris that have been eroded by the Columbia River and side streams. As you hike throughout the region you can spot some of these layers, such as at the base of Elowah Falls (No. 16) that has a 250 foot high band of the Eagle Creek Formation topped by a strip of Yakima basalt. Under those two deposits is a rock rich in a clay that becomes slippery when wet, thus promoting landslides of subsequent depositions. On the Washington side, this layer tilts 2 to 10 degrees toward the river on the Washington side, accounting, in part, for the relatively less spectacular appearance of the north slope of the Gorge. Along with continued stream deposition and basalt accumulations was more vigorous volcanic activity, resulting in such landmarks as Larch Mountain (No's. 9, 10 and 11) and Mt. Defiance (No. 33). During the most recent epoch, the forces that tear down a landscape have been, overall, greater than those that build it up. Usually, erosion is a protracted process but the examples of the massive slippage on Table Mountain on the Washington side and the considerably smaller, but still impressive, slide just below Tanner Creek Falls (No. 18) graphically illustrate that some major changes can happen quickly—a fact never to be forgotten by anyone who saw or was affected by Mt. St. Helens' May, 1980 eruption. With that abrupt loss of 1,300 feet, the current summit is no longer visible from some of the points in the Gorge where it could be seen prior to the explosion.

When the first white men—probably Lt. Broughton of the British Royal Navy and his crew who sailed up the Columbia River as far as the Sandy River in 1792—entered the Gorge, the Indians had been there for a considerable length of time. All their legends about the fiery goings-on between Wy'east (Mt. Hood) and Pa-toe (Mt. Adams) certainly must have been based on some rather impressive volcanic activity. The first documented non-natives who traversed the length of the Gorge were the members of the Lewis and Clark Expedition in 1805. After spending an exceedingly wet winter on the Oregon Coast near Astoria, they retraced their route up the Columbia the following spring. In 1810 David Thompson of The North-West Company, a Canadian fur trading firm, came down the river and camped at the present site of Cascade Locks. He also returned upstream the following year. In 1823 David Douglas, the famed botanist, explored the area behind Beacon Rock (No. 1).

Until the late 1840's, when the Barlow Road was developed over the southern flank of Mt. Hood, all settlers heading west from The Dalles had to be floated along with their belongings down the Columbia River on bateaux, a risky method of transport given the then untamed nature of the river. At that time only a faint path, seldom used even by the Indians, provided a land route through the Gorge. But beginning in the 1840's better treads were developed. In 1846 Joel Palmer, for whom Palmer Peak just south of Nesmith Point (No. 15) was named, built a pack trail along the south shore. And for river users, the then formidable rapids at the present site of Cascade Locks were circumvented on the north side in the early 1850's by a mule powered flat and a few years later a similar system was used on the Oregon side. Steam locomotives soon replaced the mules and the engine used by Joseph Ruckel (of Ruckel Ridge and Creek, No's. 24 and 25) on his south side portage was the first in the Northwest. In 1855 Ruckel and a partner started the first steamship run between Portland and his Oregon portage and, eventually, other ships extended service to The Dalles. During the last quarter of the century railroad service gradually was developed on the south side and the run on the north shore was inaugurated in 1908. Although many sections of road had been built by various people, both civilian and military, from the 1840's through the first decade of the 1900's, it was not until 1916, with the completion of the Columbia River Highway along the south side, that the entire Gorge was open to vehicular, as well as river and rail, traffic.

3

Although most of the trail building on the Oregon side of the Gorge began, reasonably enough, with the completion of the Columbia River Highway, people had been hiking the area for years before then. Earlier in the 1900's group night climbs of Larch Mountain, timed to reach the summit at sunrise, were scheduled several times a year. People then also had a penchant for ascending Larch Mountain in the dead of winter. If the weather was miserable, so much the better. Hikers would take a train to the Bridal Veil stop for Larch Mountain—or Lindsey for Mt. Defiance—and then after the climb and descent wait beside the tracks and flag down the first local that came by. Steamships also docked at suitable places from which to begin hikes. Most of the trails that now traverse the Gorge originally were built between 1915 and 1924. However, beginning in the early 1930's the majority of these routes were abandoned and many, such as the Nesmith Point, Ruckel Creek, Herman Creek (No. 27) and Starvation Ridge (No. 34) Trails, became almost impassable. However, the renaissance in hiking after the mid-1960's coupled with the presence in the Forest Service of sympathetic people like Howard Rondthaler resulted in the reopening of most of these original routes and even the rebuilding of some brand new routes, such as sections of the Gorge Trail No. 400.

HIKING IN THE COLUMBIA RIVER GORGE

Except for the three hikes that begin on the Washington side (No's. 1, 2 and 3), all the trips described in this guide are in Oregon and start from, or only a short distance off, I-84, or the Scenic Highway, the elegant precursor to the freeway. For Oregon residents doing any of those three Washington hikes it's easier to take I-84 to the Bridge of the Gods and pay the 50 cent toll rather than take Washington 14 because the latter is no freeway. However, at least once, if they haven't done so already, Oregonians should head east on Washington 14 from the Interstate Bridge at Vancouver or the I-205 Bridge because the view into the Gorge from the high point above Cape Horn is spectacular. The mileage from Portland is not given in the text because the numbered exits off I-84 indicate the distance from that city (for example, the Eagle Creek Park Exit 41 is 41 miles east of Portland). If you're approaching from the east and want to calculate driving mileages, the West Hood River exit is 62 miles from Portland. A few of the exits from I-84 are not interchanges, so on some trips you'll have to continue east a short distance to the next interchange. Mention is made in the text if this will be necessary.

An especially desirable time to visit the area is during mid to late spring. The high Cascades still are buried in snow but the Gorge is verdant with leafy deciduous trees and colorfully abundant displays of wildflowers, particularly on the lower, open slopes such as those along the Ruckel Creek, Nick Eaton (No. 29) and Starvation Ridge Trails. Late fall offers crisp air and the accents of turning maple, cottonwood, oak and dogwood. Although the latter blends with other foliage during summer, in spring perky white blooms and in fall peachy-red colored leaves spectacularly distinguish dogwood from its neighbors. Don't save Gorge—or any—hikes just for perfect weather. Some places need sunny skies to be at their best, for instance California's Sierra Nevada, but the Gorge can look just as good in gloom, rain and mist. In winter most of the low elevation Gorge trails are snow-free and, in addition to just being accessible, those in Oregon offer views of many waterfalls obscured the rest of the year by the lush foliage. However, keep track of the weather. If the Gorge has had snow or one of its infamous ice storms and there hasn't been subsequent warming, the trails may not be hikeable. Also check the forecast before heading out on winter hikes because the occasional periods of strong winds and ice can make driving and hiking extremely hazardous.

From the Columbia River to about the 1,500 foot level the woods on the Oregon side of the Gorge are a glorious blend of deciduous trees, including gnarled Oregon white oaks and giant big leaf maples, and conifers plus the lower growing vine maple, ferns, shrubs and mosses. Above that elevation the forest becomes a more simplified mix of various evergreens, including cedar, Douglas fir, hemlock and some pine. Although from west to east the woods become somewhat less lush, primarily due to a gradual decrease in rainfall, the most noticeable alteration in vegetation occurs on the Oregon side from north to south because of the abrupt change in elevation. On any hike that has considerable climbing you will pass through several distinct zones. In addition to being interesting, both visually and scientifically, these bands often tell you where you are along the hike. For example, the first clumps of beargrass indicate you're around 3,000 feet and so most of your climbing is over. As with its geologic formation, Washington did not fare quite as spectacularly as Oregon with its vegetation. Because of its gentler terrain, considerably more of the north side was logged. Also, the Yacolt Burn of 1902 devastated a considerable portion of the Washington slope. Ironically, it began near Eagle Creek on the Oregon side but violent updrafts lifted flaming debris across the river.

Amidst the verdancy of the Gorge is one plant found beside many trails below 1,000 feet that all but a few fortunate people could do without—poison oak. However, the varieties here aren't as immense as poison oak elsewhere, so if you stay on the trail you shouldn't even come in contact with it. If you are susceptible—or live with someone who is, because he can get it second hand from clothing and anything that contaminated clothing has touched—learn to recognize the plant, avoid touching it and after you return home immediately put affected clothes in the washing machine and then shower thoroughly with a strong soap. If you hike with a dog, avoid touching your pet until it's had a bath, too.

Although bear, deer and even cougar inhabit the higher areas of the Gorge, you probably won't be fortunate enough to see them, especially if you're with other people. However, you most likely will encounter smaller animals such as squirrels, chipmunks, conies and assorted birds. The only rattlesnakes you might meet on trails described in this guide would be on Dog Mountain (No. 3) from late spring through summer. Just scan the route ahead and check before you sit down. If you do encounter one dozing on the trail and you can't circumvent it, find a long stick and gently encourage it off the tread. Although only a few places in the Gorge are heavily infested with mosquitoes, such as sections of the Benson Plateau (No. 26), the area does have its animal equivalent to poison oak in the form of ticks. But they are not as prevalent as the plant, are a concern primarily in the spring and mostly inhabit the Gorge east of Horsetail Falls. While hiking, check your and your companions' clothing frequently and at home examine your entire body carefully. If you find a tick using you for a lunch counter, use tweezers to extract it with a slow, steady pull, making sure you have removed the head and front legs. To date, ticks that inhabit the area of the Gorge covered by this guide have not been found to transmit Rocky Mountain spotted fever or Lyme disease. However, if you notice any unusual symptoms after a hike, even if you haven't found a tick, consult a doctor because both of these conditions can have very serious consequences if not treated quickly. And while on the subject of illnesses, begin each hike with adequate water and carry a purification system, such as a filter, if you plan to obtain drinking water from streams along the trail. Some of the side creeks—not the major ones along which people camp and fish—that come from unvisited areas most likely are safe but any person who drinks untreated water from them should be fully aware that he's gambling.

The Oregon side of the Gorge has always supported a maze of connecting trails—only No's. 4, 18, 32 and 35 don't link up with other routes. But the recent creation of the low elevation Gorge Trail No. 400 that extends from Angels Rest (No. 5) to Wyeth (No. 31) has made even more loops and one way trips possible. To be absolutely accurate, as of early 1988, the section of No. 400 from Herman Camp (see No. 30) east to Wyeth was not completed. Almost every trail and circuit in the Gorge are described, or at least mentioned, in this guide and detailed accounts of nine Gorge routes not thoroughly covered here can be found in *50 Hiking Trails—Portland and Northwest Oregon* by Don and Roberta Lowe. The U.S. Forest Service's map *Forest Trails of the Columbia Gorge* has not been up-dated since its 1978 publication so, although providing a good overview, it does not include the many routes constructed after then. However, the Forest Service has produced a new (1987) recreation map for the entire Mt. Hood National Forest, of which the Gorge is a part. It addition to showing the boundaries of the new Columbia Wilderness, it reveals a couple of brand new trails, such as the one from the Moffett Creek Trail to Wauneka Point. Both maps are available for $1 each from ranger stations, the Mt. Hood National Forest headquarters and the Information Center of the Regional Office of the U.S. Forest Service, 319 S.W. Pine in downtown Portland. Although many backpacks can be made in the Gorge, its terrain and accessibility make it even more attractive for day hikes.

Litter is blessedly scarce but if you do see some pick it up and carry it out. Orange rinds and egg shells are organic but they decompose very slowly, so put them back in your lunch sack. Never pick wildflowers—leave them for those who follow to enjoy. Although potentially dangerous, the main reason why you should NEVER SHORTCUT SWITCHBACKS, is that doing so causes severe erosion channels that are costly to repair and Nature creates quite enough damage without help from man. These proscriptions against littering, picking wildflowers and shortcutting switchbacks are familiar but aural, as well as visual, pollution can greatly distract from the quality of an outdoor experience. Noisy people, barking dogs, radios, etc. don't belong on any trail. The Golden Rule for the outdoors is to be as inconspicuous as possible. Speaking of dogs, if you hike with one include a leash because you are required to keep your pet on it along a few trails.

Motorized travel is prohibited on all Gorge Trails and, to date, horses are allowed on only three routes: the Herman Creek Trail (No. 27), the Herman Bridge Trail, which connects the Herman Creek Trail with the Pacific Crest Trail and the PCT (No. 26), which begins from the Bridge of the Gods at Cascade Locks. If you do encounter horses on one of those three routes, stand quietly well off the trail until they have passed.

If you find any trails being misused or have questions, suggestions, complaints or compliments about how the Gorge is being administered, write to the specific agency in charge of the trail or area you're concerned about. Their addresses are listed elsewhere in this guide. Your input can be very important in determining some management decisions, so let them know what you're thinking.

The creation of the Columbia River Gorge National Scenic Area in 1986 won't mean any immediate changes but hikers can look forward to the building of new trails, particularly on the Washington side. As of 1984, the Gorge also has a Wilderness. As welcome and necessary as this permanent protection is, about the only changes hikers will note are markers identifying the boundary of the Columbia Wilderness because before the designation the 39,000 acres were being managed as a *de facto* wilderness.

Many routes in the Gorge have been reopened, rebuilt and even constructed from scratch by volunteers, for example the three paths off the Gorge Trail between Angels (No. 5) and Devils (No. 6) Rests, the Munra Point (No. 17), Tanner Creek Falls (No. 18) and Starvation Ridge (No. 34) Trails and sections of the Gorge Trail No. 400. If you're interested in being on a volunteer trail crew or have an idea for a new route that you're prepared to spend a lot of time and energy on, contact the ranger district that has jurisdiction over the area. You can help with minor maintenance on all trails you hike by removing rocks and small limbs from the tread and, the most fun, breaching the fir needle dams that have created little lakes after heavy rains.

For information on conservation matters contact the Oregon Environmental Council, 2637 S.W. Water Ave., Portland, Oregon 97201, 222-1963. If they're not directly involved in the particular issue that concerns you, they'll refer you to a group that is. Comments intended for the authors can be sent to them in care of The Touchstone Press, P.O. Box 81, Beaverton, Oregon 97075.

Good Hiking!

D.L.
R.L.

AREA MAP – *shaded areas covered by large map, pages 8-9*

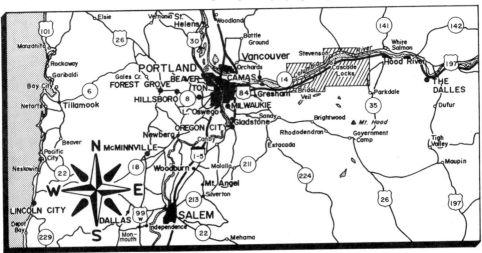

CONTENTS

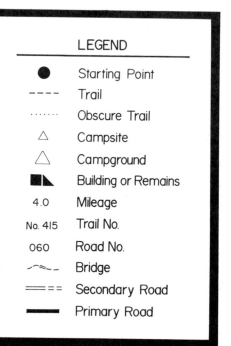

LEGEND

●	Starting Point
- - - -	Trail
....	Obscure Trail
△	Campsite
△	Campground
◼◣	Building or Remains
4.0	Mileage
No. 415	Trail No.
060	Road No.
⌒⌒	Bridge
═══	Secondary Road
▬▬	Primary Road

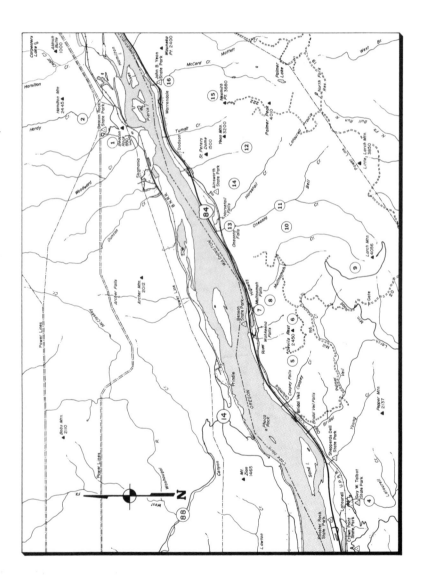

8

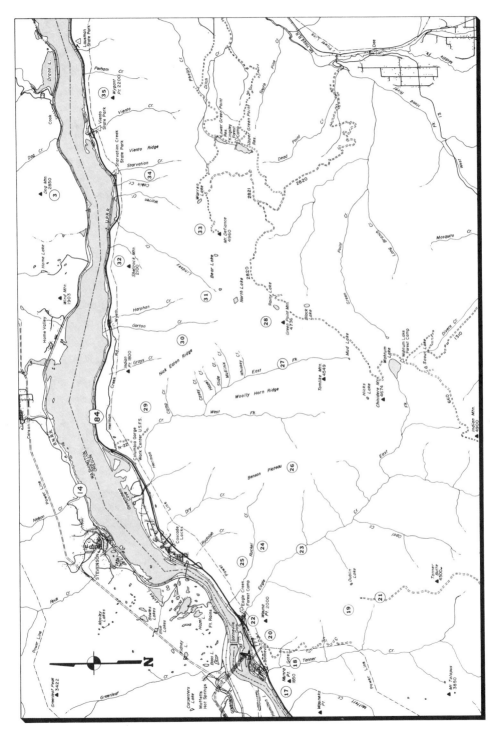

9

1 BEACON ROCK and NATURE TRAIL

One-half day trip
Distance: Beacon Rock, 0.8 mile one way
　　　　　Nature Trail, 0.7 mile one way
Elevation gain: Beacon Rock, 600 feet
　　　　　　　　Nature Trail, 150 feet;
　　　　　　　　loss 150 feet
High point: 850 feet
Allow ½ hour one way for Beacon Rock;
　　　　20 minutes one way for Nature Trail
Usually open all year (except during
　　　　　periods of severe winter weather)
Topographic map:
　　U.S.G.S. Bridal Veil, Wash.-Oreg.
　　15'　　　　　　　　　　　　　　1954

Beacon Rock, that sheer faced hulk of columnar basalt rising 850 feet above the Washington side of the Columbia River a short distance west of Bonneville Dam, is one of the most impressive and easily identified landmarks in the Gorge. Although the climbing routes tax even the most skilled, the corkscrew trail to Beacon Rock's summit, built from 1915 to 1918 by the man who then owned it, is moderately graded and made safe with catwalks and guard rails.

Because the winding ascent is relatively short, you easily can combine the climb with the Nature Trail that travels through woods and around a small lake just to the southwest of Beacon Rock's base.

Proceed on Washington 14 for 28.4 miles east of the I-205 Bridge, which is 6.2 miles east of the Interstate Bridge between Portland and Vancouver, or 6.9 miles west of the Bridge of the Gods (accessible from the Oregon side by taking the Cascade Locks Exit 44 off I-84). Leave your car in the parking area off the south shoulder in front of rest rooms or the turnout a few hundred feet west along the highway at a big clearing and the start of the possibly unsigned Nature Trail. The road up to the north goes to the start of the trail to Hamilton Mountain (No. 2), also in 4,200 acre Beacon Rock State Park.

To make the climb of Beacon Rock, walk a few hundred feet along the highway either west from the paved parking area at the rest rooms or east from the beginning of the Nature Trail to a large sign identifying the beginning of the route up Beacon Rock. Head south through woods, curve east and then begin zigzagging uphill. A gate near the beginning blocks the route when weather or other conditions make the hike unsafe. After 40 switchbacks, which become increasingly shorter, traverse around to the east side. Switch back twice, have another traverse and then make five more turns before traveling along the west side to the summit.

Understandably, the views up and down the river and of landmarks in the Gorge are extensive and engrossing. The peak above to the northeast with cliffs forming its southern face is Hamilton Mountain and Nesmith Point (No. 15) is the high point directly across the Columbia River on the Oregon side.

Originally, a bulletin board at the start of the Nature Trail displayed information on flora and fauna. Unfortunately, it was destroyed by vandals but the sign is scheduled to be replaced. Head south from the east side of the clearing, have some short ups and downs in woods and then gently descend through a more open area. Re-enter woods and continue down to the northwest end of the lake. Stay right and go around the lake. Although both its west and east ends may be swampy in early spring, quick footwork should keep your boots dry. The tread of the Nature Trail is a bit more rustic than most official routes in the Gorge and the vegetation at the east end of the lake can be dense when it's in full foliage, but traveling along less manicured routes like this has its own special charm. Evidence of beavers' work is abundant but you'll be very lucky if you actually spot any of these elusive rodents.

To complete the Nature Trail Loop, go to the junction at the northeast end of the lake, turn right and climb steeply to an old road bed. To reach a nearby viewpoint, turn right. To complete the loop, turn left (west) and travel a few yards to the junction with the trail you followed in. Turn sharply right—don't follow the path that heads northwest—and retrace your route.

Trail on Beacon Rock

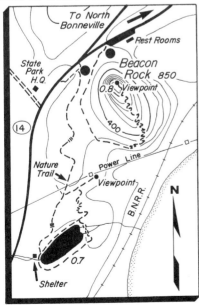

2 HAMILTON MOUNTAIN LOOP

One day trip
Distance: 3.5 miles one way (direct route);
    8 miles as a loop
Elevation gain: 2,100 feet
High point: 2,445 feet
Allow 2 hours one way for shorter route;
    4½ hours for the loop
Usually open March through November
Topographic map:
    U.S.G.S. Bridal Veil, Wash.-Oreg.
    15'   1954

Although a justifiably popular hike throughout the nine months it's usually open, the climb of Hamilton Mountain, like all trips on the Washington side of the Gorge, is especially appreciated in late fall and early spring when most of the trails on the Oregon side still are closed by snow or are mostly in perpetual shade. The loop that is possible along the upper two-thirds of the hike, even more than most circuits, offers a remarkable contrast in scenery.

Drive on Washington 14 for 28.4 miles east of the I-205 Bridge, which is 6.2 miles east the Interstate Bridge between Portland and Vancouver, or 6.9 miles west of the Bridge of the Gods (accessible from the Oregon side by taking the Cascade Locks Exit 44 off I-84). Turn north onto the road across from Beacon Rock (No. 1), as identified by the sign pointing to State Park, and follow it up 0.6 mile to a large parking area on the right. The signed Hamilton Mountain Trail begins from the north side of the lot just beyond the rest rooms.

Traverse uphill, curve left into a large basin and eventually travel under power lines, keeping right on the main trail where paths go left. The second (higher) one descends to the campground northwest of the picnic area. Enter woods and continue traversing gradually up along the wall of the bowl.

Drop slightly, cross two foot bridges and come to a side path that descends for about 100 feet to a view into the narrow, rocky gorge holding Hardy Creek. Cross a side stream, the last dependable source of water, and traverse in several short ups and downs to the junction of a spur that goes left for a few hundred feet to Pool of the Winds, a rock walled chamber at Rodney Falls. The main trail switch backs down to the bridge at the base of the falls, one of the most attractive in the Columbia Gorge, and then winds up in a few short turns to a junction. The spur on the right descends for 100 yards, losing 75 feet of elevation, to stream level at the top of Hardy Falls. The main trail continues up in six switchbacks to a fork at 1.6 miles, the lower end of the possible loop.

If you opt to make the suggested loop by following the newer (1976), more westerly leg, which is 1.5 miles longer but has a more gentle grade, stay left at the fork and traverse gradually up along the forested slope. Eventually leave the lush coniferous woods common to most of the Gorge and enter a region of deciduous growth. This area and the slopes to the west and north were devastated during the Yacolt Burn of 1902.

Meet a road, turn right, after 200 yards come to a fork and keep right again. Continue up the road for 0.8 mile to a treeless ridge crest where you'll have views of Table, Wind and Dog (No. 3) Mountains, Beacon Rock, sections of the Columbia River and Mt. Hood. Walk south along the crest of the broad ridge to an outcropping and veer right (west) onto an obvious tread. Traverse the west side of the slope, dropping slightly a few times, and then begin climbing. Switch back left, turn right at the ridge top and continue up at a more gradual grade along the narrow crest to the junction with the eastern half of the loop. To reach the summit viewpoint, keep left and walk several yards to a flat spot surrounded by bushes low enough that they don't block the view, which includes Mounts Adams and St. Helens and Bonneville Dam.

To follow the older, easterly route on the way up, keep right at the fork at 1.6 miles. Wind up in a score of mostly short switchbacks through woods to an area of cliffs called Little Hamilton Mountain, a good choice for a lunch stop when the main summit is windy. Keep left where a side path goes to a viewpoint, traverse the northwest side of the cliff area and then climb in many very short switchbacks across the open, rocky face that looks so formidable from a distance. Travel in several longer switchbacks on the sparsely wooded northwest side to the junction with the more westerly portion of the loop and turn right.

Nesmith Point from Little Hamilton Mountain

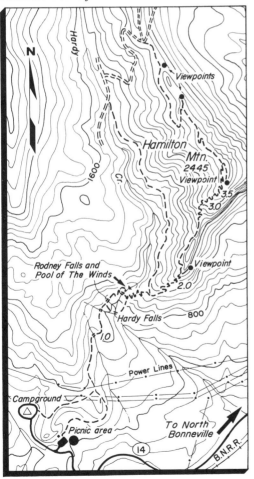

3 DOG MOUNTAIN LOOP

One day trip
Distance: 6 miles round trip for both loops
Elevation gain: 2,900 feet for both loops
High point: 2,948 feet
Allow 4 to 4½ hours round trip for both loops
Usually open March through December
Topographic map:
U.S.G.S. Mt. Defiance, Oreg.-Wash.
7.5′   1979

Although the climb of Dog Mountain has always been one of the most popular hikes in the Gorge, the opening in 1987 of a new loop to the east of the original tread between the 0.6 and 2.0 mile points plus a new loop over the summit makes a visit even better. The lower of the new routes travels at an easier grade through considerably more varied, open terrain that affords many views east up the Columbia River and south to landmarks on the Oregon side of the Gorge. The summit loop meanders over the wooded east side of the peak and then traverses the open expanses of the south slope.

The best time to visit Dog Mountain is from mid through late May when the dozens of treeless acres below the summit are smothered with the big, yellow blooms of balsamroot. However, it's one of those trails that merits repeated visits and any time in spring or fall offers rewards. Unless you like hiking in hot weather, eschew Dog Mountain in the summer but if you do make the trip from late May through the return of cool weather be on the alert for rattlesnakes by scanning the route ahead and watching where you sit. If you do encounter one snoozing on the trail and can't easily go around it, find a long stick and gently encourage it off the tread. During non-summer months carry extra clothing because a strong, nippy wind frequently blows across the summit area.

Proceed on Washington 14 for 12.8 miles east

of the Bridge of the Gods (which is accessible from the Oregon side by taking the Cascade Locks Exit 44 from I-84) to a large parking area off the north side of the highway. A sign at its east end points to the Dog Mountain Trail.

Walk east along an old road for 100 yards to a sign, turn left and follow the trail up in nine switchbacks to the south end of a grassy bench and the lower end of the new loop trail. Along this initial climb—and for most of the hike—you'll have views directly across the Columbia River to Starvation Ridge (No. 34) and micro wave tower topped Mt. Defiance (No. 33).

If you plan to take the steeper, older route up, stay straight (left) at the bench and follow the grass covered road. After a level stretch begin climbing and pass a sign pointing to water 50 feet to the east, the only source on the hike. Farther on the road narrows to a trail but the steep grade continues.

To take the new trail turn right at the bench. Very soon leave the woods and travel in semi-open country. After another stretch through timber once again have unobstructed views, with a particularly good one west past Wind Mountain and a portion of the Carson Valley to Stevenson. Walk north along a wide crest and then along a rocky little ridge before traversing in woods to the junction with the old trail at 2.0 miles. Shift to a lower gear and climb the considerably steeper grade of the old route for 0.3 mile to the last switchback at the bottom edge of the open slopes that extend from the summit. Make a long traverse to the site of a former fire lookout and the junction of the upper loop.

If you plan to make the summit loop it's recommended that you head counterclockwise. By going that direction you'll save the best until last and, if it's a warm day, you'll be climbing in shade. Stay right and traverse. The abandoned path paralleling below you is the former route of the Pacific Crest Trail, which now goes along the west and south flanks of Table Mountain and reaches Washington 14 about 100 yards west of the Bridge of the Gods (refer to No. 16 in *50 Hiking Trails—Portland and Northwest Oregon*). The open area you pass on your left just before entering woods is a good place for lunch if the summit area and the former lookout site are windy. However, check out the summit first because it can be unexpectedly calm. Soon after you begin the descent from the summit have an excellent perspective of Mt. St. Helens. Be sure to STAY ON THE OFFICIAL TRAIL—don't take any of the use paths down the fragile open slopes.

View from slopes of Dog Mountain

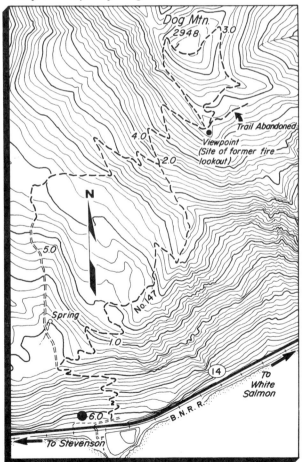

4 LATOURELL FALLS

One-half day trip
Distance: 2.1 miles round trip
Elevation gain: 550 feet
High point: 700 feet
Allow 1½ hours round trip
Usually open February through December
Topographic map:
  U.S.G.S. Bridal Veil, Wash.-Oreg.
  15'   1954

Latourell Falls is the most westerly of the many spectacular cascades on the Oregon side of the Gorge accessible from the Scenic Highway and 0.6 mile upstream from this cataract is a second, only slightly less impressive, waterfall. By making a 2.1 mile figure eight circuit you can visit both falls and with no backtracking cover all the trails in the area. Hikers who want an even easier outing can take just one of the loops and those people desiring a longer day can combine the Latourell Falls Trail with other nearby short routes, such as the Horsetail-Oneonta Creeks Loop (No. 13) and the Elowah Falls trip (No. 16).

Coming from the west proceed on I-84 to the Bridal Veil Exit 28 (not accessible to west bound traffic) and follow the exit road 0.2 mile up to its junction with the Scenic Highway. Turn right and drive west 2.9 miles to a sign stating Latourell Creek Trail and a large parking area off the south side of the road. Coming from the east, take the Ainsworth Park Exit 35 and travel west on the Scenic Highway 10.0 miles to the parking area for Latourell Falls. If you're approaching along the Scenic Highway from the west, the parking area is 2.5 miles east of Crown Point.

Climb south on the paved trail that begins several yards east from the west end of the parking area. After 200 feet come to a view of Latourell Falls, named for a prominent settler in the area, and then turn left and begin traversing up the slope of a large, wooded bowl along a now unasphalted surface. Have frequent glimpses of the falls, photogenically framed by deciduous tree limbs, make one set of switchbacks and continue up past a viewpoint to the junction of the trails that parallel each side of Latourell Creek to the upper falls.

To follow the easterly half of the loop first, keep left, climb gradually and near 0.5 mile make one set of switchbacks. Cross four small foot bridges before coming to the span at the base of the upper falls. As you begin the traverse out along the west side of the canyon walk on the level and then drop in two switchbacks. Continue downhill to the connecting trail to the bridge over Latourell Creek and the beginning of the loop you've just made. For the shortest way back to your starting point, descend to the right, cross the bridge and return along the route you followed in.

To reach the starting point without retracing your steps, keep left at the junction above the west end of the bridge and climb for 150 feet to a viewpoint. Continue up in one set of short switchbacks to a second overlook and then travel on a crest through a tunnel of deciduous growth. Traverse downhill along a stately forested slope, switch back once, pass an old water tank and wind down to the Scenic Highway on a paved section of trail.

You can walk east along the highway for 500 feet to the parking area where you started or, if you'd like a little more hiking, look for a trail heading down from the north side of the road west of the highway bridge. Follow the path down to the picnic area and then turn right at a sign pointing to Latourell Falls parking area. This picnic area and the entire region you've been hiking through are part of two adjacent State Parks, one of the relatively few parcels of public land on the Oregon side of the Gorge not under the jurisdiction of the U.S. Forest Service. Soon curve south and walk under the highway bridge whose gracefully arched supports create the effect of a massive cathedral. Continue parallel to Latourell Creek to the center of a semi-circle created by an imposing 300 foot rock wall that encloses the pool at the base of the lower falls. Cross a bridge and climb the final short distance to the parking area.

16

Latourell Falls

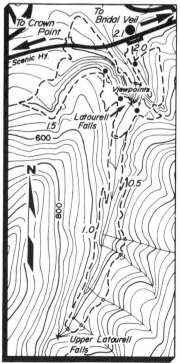

5 ANGELS REST – DEVILS REST LOOP

One day trip
Distance: 8.5 miles round trip
**   via Primrose Path**
Elevation gain: 2,600 feet
High point: 2,450 feet
Allow 5 hours round trip
Usually open April through mid December
Topographic map:
**   U.S.G.S. Bridal Veil, Wash.-Oreg.**
**   15'   1954**

Thanks to volunteer workers reopening trails and old logging roads between Angels and Devils Rests these two points can again be visited as a loop trip. For the return portion of the circuit, hikers can descend from Devils Rest along the Devils Rest Trail (No. 6) or the shorter Primrose Path and then head back to Angels Rest along Trail No. 415. People wanting a short outing can just go the 2.3 miles to the large, flat summit area of Angels Rest and leisurely enjoy the superb views of the western end of the Gorge and down river toward Portland. Shuttle fanciers have the options of ending at Wahkeena Falls or continuing by one of three routes to Multnomah Falls (No's. 7 and 8).

From the west drive on I-84 to the Bridal Veil Exit 28 (not accessible to west bound traffic) and follow the exit road 0.2 mile up to its junction with the Scenic Highway. Leave your car in the large parking area between the two roads. If you're approaching from the east, take the Ainsworth Park Exit 35 and follow the Scenic Highway for 7.1 miles. Coming from the west along the Scenic Highway, the trailhead is 5.3 miles east of Crown Point.

Cross the Scenic Highway to the possibly un-signed trail traversing east up a bank. Walk through lush woods, switch back twice and then traverse a rocky swath where you can see down to the Columbia River and across it to the cliffs of Cape Horn. Pass a short spur that goes to a view of Coopey Falls, travel parallel to Coopey Creek and then cross it on a bridge. Continue up in switchbacks and traverses, farther on alternating between the north and south sides of a ridge. At 2.0 miles walk along an open, rocky area with brushy vegetation. Switch back and come to a narrow crest and the unsigned junction of the path out to Angels Rest. To reach this overlook, stay straight (left), have an easy scramble over a few rocks and travel northwest along the ridge top for a few hundred feet.

To continue the hike to Devils Rest, head southeast at the junction on the narrow crest, curve around the head of the basin and climb through woods in two short switchbacks. Fifty yards beyond the final turn come to the signed west end of Fox Glove Way. If you're making the suggested loop, it's recommended that you follow this route up and return along No. 415 (concurrently, the Gorge Trail No, 400).

Fox Glove Way climbs moderately through woods to an old logging road and then heads back to Trail No. 415. To continue directly to Devils Rest, turn right at the logging road onto signed Upper Fox Glove Way. Farther on begin traveling on a narrower tread, eventually veer left onto an old road and after 100 feet come to a T-junction at a wider road. Turn left and walk slightly downhill along the bed for 0.3 mile to a sign on the right marking the Devils Fork Trail. Leave the road and climb along a path for another 0.3 mile to the junction with the Devils Rest Trail. Turn left and in several yards come to the base of Devils Rest's little summit knoll.

If you plan to return along the shorter Primrose Path, follow the tread that heads to the right (east) around the base of the summit knoll and soon begin descending to the north along a rustic tread to Trail No. 415.

Turn left, cross two bridges and continue gradually up to the east end of Fox Glove Way. It is a trail for 0.1 mile as it wends through a superb grove of tall alder and then follows an old logging road for 0.5 mile to the junction with Upper Fox Glove Way.

From the east end of Fox Glove Way, Trail No. 415 continues traversing and then drops steeply for a short distance to a stream crossing at a picnic and camp area. Walk on the level, climb slightly and eventually come to the junction of the west end of Fox Glove Way.

Aerial view of Angels Rest

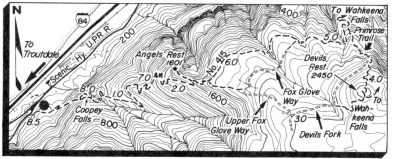

6 WAHKEENA – DEVILS REST LOOP

One day trip
Distance: 6.8 miles round trip
Elevation gain: 2,500 feet
High point: 2,450 feet
Allow 4 to 4½ hours round trip
Usually open April through mid December
Topographic map:
   U.S.G.S. Bridal Veil, Wash.-Oreg.
   15'   1954

Unlike the spacious and open setting of aptly named Angels Rest (No. 5), the dense woods and scattered rock outcroppings at Devils Rest make it a more appropriate place for elves and other fairy folk than the Devil. The lower part of the hike passes two impressive waterfalls and the suggested loop down from Devils Rest is along the enchantingly rustic Primrose Path. Refer to No's. 5, 7 and 8 for details of other possible return loops.

Approaching from the west, take I-84 to the Bridal Veil Exit 28 (not accessible to west bound traffic) and follow the exit road 0.2 mile up to the junction with the Scenic Highway. This junction is 5.3 miles east of Crown Point along the Scenic Highway. Head east along the Scenic Highway 2.6 miles to the parking area at Wahkeena Falls. Coming from the east, take the Ainsworth Park Exit 35 and continue west on the Scenic Highway for 4.5 miles.

The trail begins just above the south side of the road at the west end of the bridge over Wahkeena Creek. Switch back once and traverse up along the side of the canyon to Wahkeena Falls. Continue a short distance farther, now on an unpaved surface, to the junction of the Perdition Trail No. 421 to Multnomah Falls, turn right and climb in 10 more switchbacks to a crest. Turn left and walk 50 feet along the ridge top to a four way junction where the short spur to

the right goes down to Necktie Falls and the one left heads up to Monument Viewpoint.

Keep straight, cross Wahkeena Creek twice on little foot bridges and wind up in several short switchbacks to the ford of the small stream at the base of Fairy Falls. Make five more turns up to the junction of the Vista Point Trail No. 419, an alternate route to the lower end of the Devils Rest Trail. If you intend to take the Primrose Path down from the summit but do not plan to make one of the possible loops by Multnomah Creek, the recommended itinerary is to take the Vista Point Trail up. If you opt to do this, turn left, after several yards cross Fairy Creek and climb to the crest of the ridge where an unsigned little loop goes downslope. Continue mostly uphill to the junction with the Wahkeena Trail. Turn left and walk 75 feet to the beginning of the trail to Devils Rest.

To follow the Wahkeena Trail from the junction above Fairy Falls, turn right and climb to the junction with the Angels Rest Trail No. 415. Turn left, staying on No. 420, and traverse steadily uphill for 0.4 mile, pass the upper end of the Vista Point Trail and 75 feet farther come to the Devils Rest Trail on your right.

Climb in seven irregular switchbacks and then follow along the breaks where you can see ahead to Devils Rest. Stay straight (right) at the signed connector to Multnomah Basin Road and continue on the level. Have a short drop and then mostly climb past paths to two viewpoints. The second one provides an even more extensive view that includes many Gorge landmarks plus Mounts Rainier and Adams. Continue climbing and travel along a short section of an old, overgrown road bed before curving up to the right and going the final several hundred feet to Devils Rest. The signed Devils Fork Trail on your left several yards before the little summit knoll is described in No. 5.

To make the highly recommended return loop, follow the path to the right around the base of the summit knoll and soon begin descending to the north along a rough tread. Where you come to a steep drop-off follow the route to the left (the one to the right soon dead ends) and continue moderately steeply downhill through a variety of woods. Where you meet No. 415, which doubles as a section of the Gorge Trail No. 400 and connects Angels Rest and the Wahkeena Trail, turn right, soon begin a series of six switchbacks and then travel briefly beside Wahkeena Creek. Pass Wahkeena Spring, a good spot for a snack stop, and 100 yards farther come to the Wahkeena Trail.

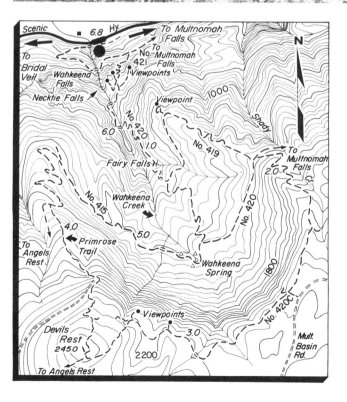

7 MULTNOMAH – PERDITION LOOP

One-half day trip
Distance: 3.1 miles round trip
Elevation gain: 1,000 feet
High point: 900 feet
Allow 2 hours round trip
Usually open February through December
Topographic map:
  U.S.G.S. Bridal Veil, Wash.-Oreg.
  15'   1954

Combining the maps for the Multnomah–Perdition and the Multnomah–Wahkeena (No. 8) Loops reveals three main routes between Multnomah and Wahkeena Creeks with several attendant spurs to viewpoints. Indeed, it is the densest network of trails in the Gorge and you could spend two delightful sessions untangling this exceptionally scenic knot.

Actually, all the trails between Multnomah and Wahkeena Falls could be covered in one day but this area lends itself to a more leisurely pace with unhurried stops at all the overlooks and other points of interest. Generous sprinklings of vine maple, dogwood and other deciduous vegetation make the area particularly attractive in late fall. Throughout the year, these popular trails are less crowded on week days.

Drive on I-84 to the Multnomah Falls Exit 31 and leave your car in the parking area. Go through the pedestrian tunnel under the freeway and cross the Scenic Highway. You also could reach this point along the Scenic Highway by taking it east 3.1 miles from the Bridal Veil Exit 28 off I-84 (not accessible to westbound traffic) or 4.0 miles west from the Ainsworth Park Exit 35.

From the east side of the stone restaurant and gift shop follow a series of steps and platforms and then wind up on a wide, paved trail to the bridge above Lower Multnomah Falls. Cross the span, go out of the side canyon and traverse along the wall of the Gorge. The Ak-Wanee Trail that heads east at the first switchback is one segment of the Gorge Trail No. 400 and meets the Oneonta Trail (No. 11) in 2.0 miles.

Turn right at the junction of the Ak-Wanee Trail, continuing on the paved surface, and wind up in almost one dozen more switchbacks to a crest. Descend briefly and come to the short spur that heads right (west) to the overlook at the top of Multnomah Falls. The main trail, which is now unpaved, crosses a bridge over Multnomah Creek and several yards farther comes to the junction of the Perdition Trail. The Multnomah Creek Trail (No. 9) continues south, passing the east end of the Wahkeena Trail (No. 8) after 0.7 mile, farther on the lower end of the Franklin Ridge Trail (No. 10) and eventually a connector to the Oneonta Trail before reaching Larch Mountain.

Turn right onto the Perdition Trail and travel above Multnomah Creek until the stream curves right and becomes Multnomah Falls. Continue traversing to a spur on your right that heads downslope to a viewpoint. Descend gradually along the main trail, cross a footbridge and begin dropping more noticeably. As the grade levels off keep left where a dead end path angles back to the right.

Climb a short distance and pass a trail on your right that goes to a high viewpoint. Not surprisingly, from these overlooks you'll have views directly down onto the area around Multnomah Falls Lodge and across the Columbia River to landmarks on the Washington side of the Gorge. Continue up the spine of a small ridge and walk along its summit before descending on long, wide steps. Wend through a delicate sylvan setting to a steep stairway and from its lower end traverse for 0.1 mile to the junction with the Wahkeena Trail. (It eventually connects with the routes to Angels (No. 5) and Devils (No. 6) Rests and loops back to the Multnomah Creek Trail.)

Stay right and continue traversing, resume traveling on a paved surface and cross the stone bridge near the base of Wahkeena Falls. Traverse down, switch back once and come to just above the Scenic Highway.

To complete the loop back to Multnomah Falls, cross the little wooden bridge over Wahkeena Creek, then a smaller span and continue heading east for 0.5 mile, mostly contouring in woods as you travel parallel to—but well above—the Scenic Highway.

Multnomah Falls

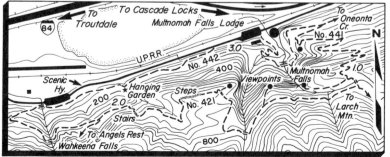

8 MULTNOMAH – WAHKEENA LOOP

One day trip
Distance: 5.4 miles round trip
Elevation gain: 1,650 feet
High point: 1,600 feet
Allow 3 hours round trip
Usually open February through December
Topographic map:
U.S.G.S. Bridal Veil, Wash.-Oreg.
15'   1954

The Wahkeena Trail is the highest of the three interconnecting routes between Multnomah and Wahkeena Creeks. The most visually interesting of the possible loops combines the Wahkeena Trail, which follows the most scenic sections of Multnomah and Wahkeena Creeks and traverses slopes of exceptionally attractive, almost parklike, woods, and the middle, viewpoint-laden Perdition Trail (No. 7). However, hikers who want a shorter outing can return along the lowest of the three treads, No. 422, which parallels just above the Scenic Highway. If you're intending to combine either the Perdition or the Wahkeena Trails with No. 422, it doesn't make any difference which route you do first or whether you begin at Multnomah or Wahkeena Falls. The written description starts from Multnomah Falls and heads clockwise but the mileage shown on the map reflects a beginning point at Wahkeena Falls and a counterclockwise orientation.

Proceed on I-84 to the Multnomah Falls Exit 31 and leave your car in the parking area. Go through the pedestrian tunnel under the freeway and cross the Scenic Highway. You also could reach this point along the Scenic Highway by taking it east 3.1 miles from the Bridal Veil Exit 28 off I-84 (not accessible to westbound traffic) or 4.0 miles west from the Ainsworth Park Exit 35.

From the east side of the stone restaurant and gift shop follow a series of steps and platforms and then wind up on a wide, paved trail to the bridge above Lower Multnomah Falls. Cross the span, go out of the side canyon and traverse along the wall of the Gorge. Continue on the paved surface at the first switchback, where the Ak-Wanee Trail continues east, and wind up in almost one dozen more turns to a crest. Descend briefly and come to the short spur to the overlook at the top of Multnomah Falls. The main trail, which is now unpaved, crosses a bridge over Multnomah Creek and several yards farther comes to the junction of the Perdition Trail. Stay left, travel gradually up beside Multnomah Creek and walk under a rock overhang just before coming near the base of Upper Multnomah Falls. Wind up in several short switchbacks and then traverse to the junction of the Wahkeena Trail several hundred yards before a high bridge over Multnomah Creek. (The Multnomah Creek Trail continues to Larch Mountain, No's. 9, 10 and 11).

Turn right, traverse uphill and curve onto the north facing slope. Cross small Shady Creek, pass the lower end of the Devils Rest Trail (No. 6) and 75 feet farther come to the upper end of the Vista Point Trail No. 419 that rejoins the Wahkeena Trail just above Fairy Falls. (If you don't opt to follow the Vista Point Trail down this time around, be sure to take this scenic route on some future hike.) To continue on the Wahkeena Trail, keep straight (left) and descend to the junction of Trail No. 415 to Angels Rest (No. 5). A good place for a snack stop is about 100 yards west along the Angels Rest Trail at Wahkeena Spring.

To continue the Multnomah-Wahkeena Loop, turn right (north) at the junction of No. 415 and descend on No. 420. After a few turns pass the lower end of the Vista Point Trail, make five more short switchbacks and ford the stream at the base of Fairy Falls. Continue down the narrowing gorge, cross Wahkeena Creek twice on bridges and come to a four-way junction. The spur to the left descends for 0.1 mile, losing 200 feet of elevation, to a fenced ledge at the lip of Necktie Falls and the path to the right climbs 0.1 mile to Monument Viewpoint above Benson State Park.

The main trail continues north along the crest from the four-way junction for 50 feet and then curves sharply right and begins winding downhill. At the eleventh switchback come to the junction of the Perdition Trail. The Wahkeena Trail turns left, passes Wahkeena Falls and then drops to the Scenic Highway. Take it to make the easier return route, which is 2.5 miles shorter and involves 1,000 fewer feet of uphill than returning along the Perdition Trail.

To return along the Perdition Trail, stay right at the bottom of the switchbacks and head east.

Fairy Falls

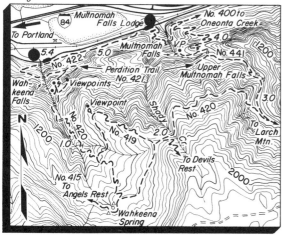

9 MULTNOMAH CREEK TRAIL to LARCH MOUNTAIN

One day trip or backpack
Distance: 7 miles one way
Elevation gain: 4,100 feet
High point: 4,055 feet
Allow 4 hours one way
Usually open May through November
Topographic map:
  U.S.G.S. Bridal Veil, Wash.-Oreg.
  15'   **1954**

The Multnomah Creek Trail is the most westerly, direct and popular of the three routes that head more or less straightaway up to Larch Mountain. From Sherrard Point on the summit the view extends from the Three Sisters in the central Oregon Cascades to Washington's Mt. Rainier. You can make a loop by combining the Multnomah Creek Trail with the Franklin Ridge Trail (No. 10) or the Oneonta Trail (No. 11). The former is a perfect loop but the latter necessitates establishing a short car shuttle or hiking 2.0 miles along the Gorge Trail No. 400. For an easier circuit you can take the route that connects the Franklin Ridge and Multnomah Creek Trails just above their respective midway points. You also can follow this connector to make a shorter loop on the Oneonta Trail. Or, you can take the upper 3.0 miles of the Oneonta Trail as a loop. Because a paved road goes to the summit of Larch Mountain, you also could do the hike one way only.

Drive on I-84 to the Multnomah Falls Exit 31. Go through the pedestrian tunnel under the freeway and cross the Scenic Highway. You also can reach this point by taking the Scenic Highway east 3.1 miles from the Bridal Veil Exit 28 (not accessible to west bound traffic) or 4.0 miles west from the Ainsworth Park Exit 35.

From the east side of the stone restaurant and gift shop follow a series of steps and platforms and then wind up on a wide, paved trail to the bridge above Lower Multnomah Falls. Cross it, traverse out of the canyon and then head east along the wall of the Gorge. At the first switch-back pass the Ak-Wanee Trail, a section of the Gorge Trail No. 400, and continue winding up in almost one dozen more turns. Go over a crest and descend, coming to the end of the paved surface at the junction of the spur to the overlook at the top of Multnomah Falls. Stay on the main trail, cross a bridge over Multnomah Creek and several yards beyond the span meet the junction of the Perdition Trail (No. 7). Stay left and travel beside a particularly attractive section of Multnomah Creek to near the base of Upper Multnomah Falls. Wind up in a series of short switchbacks and traverse beyond the top of the falls to the east end of the Wahkeena Trail (No. 8).

Stay straight (left) and after several hundred yards recross Multnomah Creek on a high bridge. Traverse 0.4 mile to the junction of the High and Low Water Trails. (At this fork note the route that heads in a downstream direction below the main trail so you don't inadvertently follow it on the return.) You can see if the Low Water Trail, which is shorter and involves no climbing, is feasible by walking along it for several yards and peering around the corner. If you take the upper route, stay right at the path to Multnomah Basin. Two-tenths mile beyond where the High and Low Water Trails merge come to the Multnomah Basin Road. Cross it and after 0.3 mile come to the junction of the Franklin Ridge Trail.

Stay right (straight) and several hundred yards farther cross the East Fork of Multnomah Creek on a bridge. Make two short switchbacks and after 0.5 mile cross Multnomah Creek, also on a bridge. Head downstream and then switch back and resume heading south. One-tenth mile from the turn traverse a large talus slope, re-enter woods and continue up to the junction of the Multnomah Creek Way Trail No. 444 that connects with the Franklin Ridge and Oneonta Trails.

Keep straight (right), farther on come to a section of rougher tread and then level off and pass the site of a former shelter just before coming to a spur from the Larch Mountain Road. Cross it and resume climbing along the now mostly smooth trail. Farther on you'll glimpse the rocky face of Sherrard Point.

Near the summit skirt the edge of the picnic area, pass rest rooms and come to the southwest corner of the parking area at the end of Larch Mountain Road. Walk to the northwest corner of the turnaround and follow the trail that begins there for 0.2 mile to Sherrard Point and those extensive views.

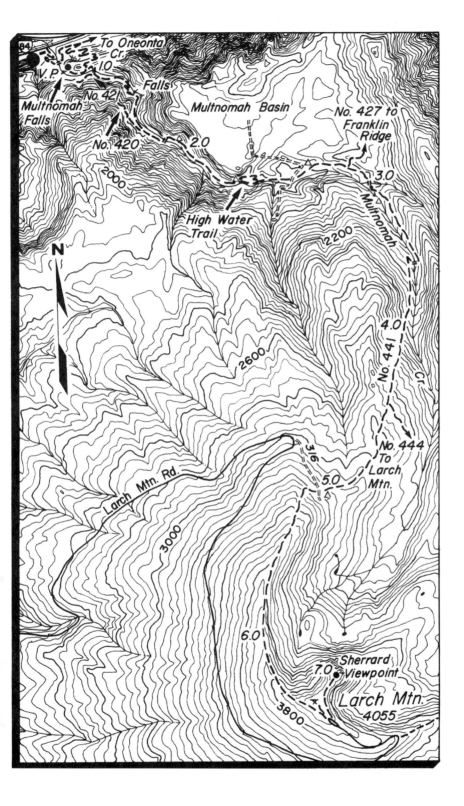

To Oneonta Cr.

V.P.

No. 421

Falls

.10

Multnomah Falls

No. 420

2.0

Multnomah Basin

No. 427 to Franklin Ridge

3.0

High Water Trail

2000

2200

N

2600

Multnomah Cr.

4.0

No. 441

No. 444 To Larch Mtn.

Larch Mtn. Rd.

3.16

5.0

3000

6.0

7.0 ● Sherrard Viewpoint

3800

Larch Mtn. 4055

10 FRANKLIN RIDGE TRAIL to LARCH MOUNTAIN

One day trip or backpack
Distance: 9.1 miles one way
Elevation gain: 4,200 feet; loss 160 feet
High point: 4,055 feet
Allow 5½ to 6 hours one way
Usually open May through November
Topographic map:
  U.S.G.S. Bridal Veil, Wash.-Oreg.
  15'   1954

The Franklin Ridge Trail is the middle of the three relatively direct routes to Larch Mountain (No's. 9, 10 and 11) and, everything considered, the most varied. In addition to the section along the best looking stretch of Multnomah Creek, the Franklin Ridge Trail travels through a variety of exceptionally attractive woods and passes several viewpoints before reaching the panoramic overlook on the summit of Larch Mountain. Refer to No. 9 for details on the many possible loops.

Proceed on I-84 to the Multnomah Falls Exit 31. Go through the pedestrian tunnel under the freeway and cross the Scenic Highway. You also can reach this point by taking the Scenic Highway east 3.1 miles from the Bridal Veil Exit 28 (not accessible to west bound traffic) or 4.0 miles west from the Ainsworth Park Exit 35.

From the east side of the stone restaurant and gift shop follow a series of steps and platforms and then wind up on a wide, paved trail to the bridge above Lower Multnomah Falls. Cross it, traverse out of the canyon and then head east along the wall of the Gorge. At the first switchback pass the Ak-Wanee Trail, a section of the Gorge Trail No. 400, and continue winding up in almost one dozen more turns. Go over a crest and descend, coming to the end of the paved surface at the junction of the spur to the overlook at the top of Multnomah Falls. Stay on the main trail, cross a bridge over Multnomah Creek and several yards beyond the span meet the junction of the Perdition Trail (No. 7). Stay left, travel beside Multnomah Creek and near the base of Upper Multnomah Falls wind up in a series of short switchbacks. Traverse beyond the top of the falls to the east end of the Wahkeena Trail (No. 8).

Stay straight (left) and after several hundred yards recross Multnomah Creek on a high bridge. Traverse 0.4 mile to the junction of the High and Low Water Trails. If you take the upper route, stay right at a possibly unsigned path to Multnomah Basin. Two-tenths mile beyond where the High and Low Water Trails merge come to the Multnomah Basin Road. Cross it and after 0.3 mile come to the signed junction of the Franklin Ridge Trail.

Turn left, go over a low crest and travel along the southeastern edge of Multnomah Basin. Traverse up a wooded slope to a large meadow where the trail turns right and for the next mile climb along the top of a sometimes narrow ridge. The lower portion of this crest is park-like with a mix of deciduous and evergreen trees shading an abundance of sorrel and wildflowers. Pass through a small clearing and farther on have views east to Nesmith Point (No. 15) and across the Columbia River to Table Mountain and beyond to Mt. Adams. Leave the crest near 4.5 miles and traverse through woods of especially large conifers to the junction of the Oneonta Trail. Keep straight (right) on No. 424, soon drop slightly and wind through a corridor of cleared blowdown. Have two sets of short climbs and descents to a junction.

Turn right onto Trail No. 446 and descend about 250 yards to an easy ford of the East Fork of Multnomah Creek. Resume climbing, travel along a ridge crest and then descend to the junction of Multnomah Creek Way Trail No. 444 that heads west 0.2 mile to the Multnomah Creek Trail No. 441. Turn left, following the sign to the Oneonta Trail, and soon pass near a large meadow. Begin winding up along a rooty, rocky trail and then resume climbing on a smoother tread. Come to an old logging railroad bed and follow its gentle grade up for 0.5 mile to the junction with the Oneonta Trail. Turn right and continue climbing for another 0.8 mile to the Larch Mountain Road. Turn right and follow it up 0.4 mile to the northwest corner of the parking area and the start of the 0.2 mile spur out to the superb viewpoint at Sherrard Point.

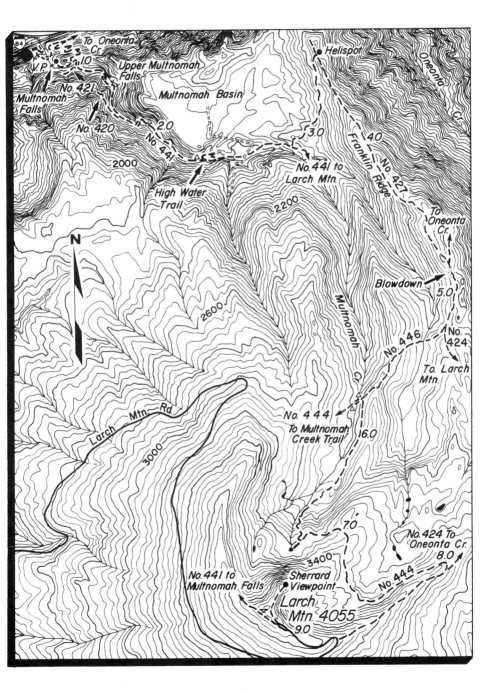

To Oneonta Cr.

Helispot

84

V.P.

Upper Multnomah Falls

No. 421

Multnomah Basin

No. 420

Multnomah Falls

No. 441

2.0

High Water Trail

2000

No. 441 to Larch Mtn.

3.0

Franklin Ridge

No. 427

4.0

To Oneonta Cr.

2200

N

2600

Multnomah Cr.

Blowdown

5.0

No. 446

No. 424

To Larch Mtn.

Larch Mtn. Rd.

3000

No. 444

To Multnomah Creek Trail

6.0

7.0

3400

No. 424 To Oneonta Cr.

8.0

No. 444

No. 441 to Multnomah Falls

Sherrard Viewpoint

Larch Mtn. 4055

9.0

11 ONEONTA TRAIL to LARCH MOUNTAIN

One day trip or backpack
Distance: 8.4 miles one way
Elevation gain: 4,300 feet; loss 250 feet
High point: 4,075 feet
Allow 5 to 5½ hours one way
Usually open May through November
Topographic map:
U.S.G.S. Bridal Veil, Wash.-Oreg.
15'   1954

With the exceptions of No's. 4, 18, 32 and 35 all the routes on the Oregon side of the Gorge interconnect and the Oneonta Trail is among those that provide a particularly large number of options. Two of the most obvious are returning from Larch Mountain along the Multnomah Creek (No. 9) or Franklin Ridge (No. 10) Trails. Most people would chose to establish a short car shuttle for either of these but they could take the Gorge Trail No. 400 back to the starting point. An especially interesting return route, just re-opened in 1987, is along the Bell Creek Trail that heads east and north from the Oneonta Trail about 2.0 miles below Larch Mountain to the Horsetail Creek Trail (No. 12), which connects with the Oneonta Trail at the latter's 2.9 mile point. Because a paved road goes to the summit of Larch Mountain, you could establish a car shuttle and do the hike one way only.

Proceed on the Scenic Highway 5.2 miles east from its junction with the road up from the Bridal Veil Exit 28 off I-84 (not accessible to west bound traffic) or 1.9 miles west from the Ainsworth Park Exit 35 to a wide spot for parking on the north side of the road and a sign on the south that identifies the beginning of the Oneonta Trail. This trailhead is 2.1 miles east of Multnomah Falls and 0.5 miles west of Horsetail Falls.

Traverse west up to a switchback. The trail that continues west here is a section of the Gorge Trail No. 400. Turn left and continue up to a crest

where a side path goes to three viewpoints. Cross a scree slope inhabited by conies and travel along the wall of Oneonta Creek canyon to the junction of Trail No. 438 (No. 13). Stay straight and continue along the forested canyon wall. Make one set of switchbacks and then begin descending just before the first sighting of Triple Falls. Wind down, staying right at the short spur to a viewpoint and soon cross Oneonta Creek on a bridge. Parallel the stream through an especially lush area, make two sets of switchbacks separated by a traverse and 0.4 mile beyond the last turn recross Oneonta Creek on a bridge. Climb in two short switchbacks to the junction of the Horsetail Creek Trail No. 425.

Keep right, soon climb through an open, rocky area and then begin a long traverse to the northwest. Wind up very steeply, curve onto an east facing slope and climb at a more moderate grade. At the end of one of the several rocky swaths you cross make a set of switchbacks and pass viewpoints over the upper portion of Oneonta canyon. Have one final series of four steep switchbacks to a broad wooded crest uncharacteristically void of ground cover and descend briefly to the junction of the Franklin Ridge Trail No. 427.

Turn left, drop slightly and wind through a corridor of cleared blowdown from the infamous 1962 Columbus Day storm. Climb and descend twice for short distances before walking gradually uphill to the junction of Trail No. 446 that connects with No. 444 (refer to No. 10). Stay left, climb over a small crest and make two short descents separated by a gradual stretch to a ford. Climb and then descend slightly to the junction of the Bell Creek Trail.

Keep right and traverse up along a new portion of the Oneonta Trail that was realigned when the western end of Bell Creek Trail was re-built. Cross an old road and after 0.2 mile come to the junction of the upper end of Trail No. 444. Stay straight (left) and continue up for 0.8 mile through increasingly open terrain to the Larch Mountain Road. Turn right and walk up it 0.4 mile to its end and the 0.2 spur that heads from the northwest corner of the parking area to the excellent overlook at Sherrard Point.

From its upper end the Bell Creek Trail traverses gradually downhill for 1.2 miles to the large area of blowdown that was the major obstacle to getting the route re-opened. At the north end of the cleared area begin traveling on the original alignment and follow it at a mostly gradual uphill grade to the junction with the Horsetail Creek Trail.

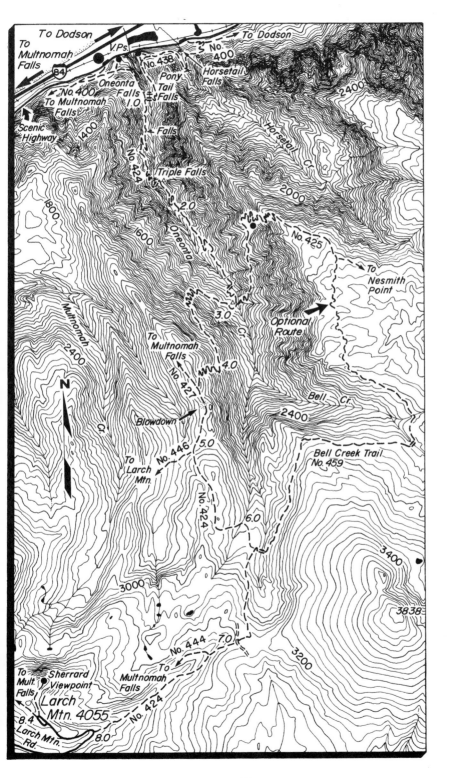

12 HORSETAIL CREEK TRAIL

One day trip or backpack
Distance: 8.4 miles one way
Elevation gain: 4,100 feet; loss 350 feet
High point: 3,871 feet
Allow 5 to 6 hours one way
Usually open June through November
Topographic map:
   U.S.G.S. Bridal Veil, Wash.-Oreg.
   15′   **1954**

The east-west oriented Horsetail Creek Trail connects the Oneonta (No. 11) and Nesmith Point (No. 15) Trails so it's ideal for a car shuttle. One of two possible loops would be to take the Oneonta Trail 6.2 miles up to the recently (1987) reopened Bell Creek Trail and follow the latter to the 5.0 mile point of the Horsetail Creek Trail. This circuit involves a little over 3,000 feet of climbing and a total distance of 15 miles. Hikers who enjoy very steep uphill along use paths can take the Rock of Ages Ridge route (No. 14) up to the 6.7 mile point of the Horsetail Creek Trail and return along the latter. This entire loop is 9.7 miles and also involves 3,000 feet of uphill. Later in the hiking season you will hardly get the soles of your boots wet on the fords of Oneonta Creek at 3.0 miles and the three forks of Horsetail Creek but from spring through early summer the crossings, especially the one of Oneonta Creek, though definitely not impassable, are more of a problem.

Proceed on the Scenic Highway 5.7 miles east of the junction of the road up from the Bridal Veil Exit 28 off I-84 (not accessible to west bound traffic) or 1.4 miles west from the Ainsworth Park Exit 35 to the large parking area at Horsetail Falls.

Climb to the east and continue up in five switchbacks. The Gorge Trail No. 400 heads east at the third turn. Beyond the final switchback walk west along the cliff face and as you curve into the canyon holding Ponytail Falls pass the unsigned Rock of Ages use path heading up the side of the ridge. Walk behind the falls, traverse out of the canyon and then travel on the level to a fork. The branch to the right passes an overlook before rejoining the main trail. Traverse along the east side of Oneonta Creek canyon and then wind down in six little switchbacks to a bridge. Climb in one set of switchbacks to the Oneonta Trail and turn left.

Climb gently along the west side of the gorge, make one set of switchbacks and begin descending at the first sighting of Triple Falls. Stay right at a short path to a viewpoint and soon cross Oneonta Creek on a new bridge. Parallel the stream through an especially lush area, make two sets of switchbacks separated by a traverse and 0.4 mile beyond the final turn recross Oneonta Creek on another new bridge. Climb in two short switchbacks to the junction of the Horsetail Creek Trail.

Turn left, descend slightly and ford Oneonta Creek. Wind up in several short switchbacks, have a little drop to a stream and then continue up to another one. Early in the season you'll pass a few more flows along this traverse. Climb in nine switchbacks and after a traverse pass a short spur to a nubbin on your right where you'll have views across the densely forested upper end of Oneonta Creek canyon to Larch Mountain (No's. 9, 10 and 11). Continue corkscrewing up in six more switchbacks and then begin hiking at an increasingly gradual grade. A short distance beyond where the trail almost levels off come to the junction of the Bell Creek Trail.

Stay straight (left) and 0.7 mile from the junction of the Bell Creek Trail cross the West Fork of Horsetail Creek. Traverse out of the side canyon holding the stream and climb slightly to the ford of the Middle Fork of Horsetail Creek. Continue uphill and then descend briefly to the East Fork of Horsetail Creek. Wind through a more open area of deciduous growth and rise moderately to the unsigned junction of the Rock of Ages Ridge route on your left.

Keep straight (right) and walk for 0.3 mile near the rim of the Gorge. Go over the shoulder of Yeon Mountain and continue gradually uphill, again near the rim, to an overlook at 7.9 miles directly across from Beacon Rock (No. 1) and Hamilton Mountain (No. 2). Veer away from the edge and drop slightly to Road 222. If you plan to return along the Nesmith Point Trail refer to No. 15.

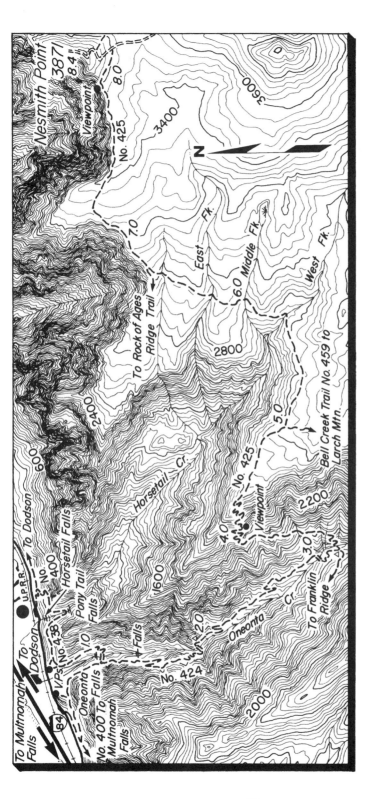

13 HORSETAIL CREEK – ONEONTA CREEK LOOP

One-half day trip
Distance: 2.7 miles round trip
Elevation gain: 500 feet
High point: 400 feet
Allow 1½ hours round trip
Usually open February through December
Topographic map:
  U.S.G.S. Bridal Veil, Wash.-Oreg.
  15'   1954

This scenic and charming loop is justifiably one of the most popular short trips in the Gorge. Beginning at impressive Horsetail Falls, it goes through a cavern behind Ponytail Falls, passes overlooks, peers into the narrow chasm of Oneonta Gorge and traverses a rocky slope inhabited by conies all the while winding through the attractive woods characteristic of the area.

Drive on the Scenic Highway 5.7 miles east of the junction of the road up from the Bridal Veil Exit 28 off I-84 (not accessible to westbound traffic) or 1.4 miles west from the Ainsworth Park Exit 35 to the large parking area at Horsetail Falls. A big wooden sign with a trail map of the area identifies the start of the hike.

Climb to the east and continue up in five switchbacks. Heading east from the third turn is the Gorge Trail No. 400, the low level route that, to date, extends from Angels Rest (No. 5) to Herman Camp (No. 30) and soon will continue east to Wyeth (No. 31). Exploring this section of the Gorge Trail and/or the one you pass at the 2.1 mile point are fun extensions of the loop. Beyond the final switchback contour west along the face of the moss, fern and wildflower dotted rock face and as you curve into the canyon holding Ponytail Falls pass the unsigned Rock of Ages Ridge use path (No. 14) heading up the side of the ridge. Walk behind the falls

in a wide, low ceilinged chamber. The rock here, weaker than the layers above and below, has been more susceptible to erosion by freezing and thawing and flowing water. Traverse out of the side canyon and once again walk on the level along the face of the Gorge. Where the trail forks you can follow either branch. The path to the right passes a view of the Columbia River and a backwash area of grass and cottonwoods before rejoining the main route.

Traverse gradually down along the east wall of Oneonta Creek canyon and then descend in six short switchbacks to the bridge across the defile. You'll have a particularly interesting view down the narrow gorge at the second turn. The origin of this canyon is the same as the cavern behind Ponytail Falls except here the weaker rock is in a vertical instead of a horizontal configuration. Climb in one set of switchbacks to the Oneonta Trail (No. 11). (Another possible side trip is to head up this route for 0.7 mile to Triple Falls.)

To complete the loop, turn right and climb gradually along the west slope of the canyon. Curve west and as you traverse a rocky swath you may see conies, or at least hear their distinctive bleating sound. These shy, adorable looking rodents don't hibernate and through the winter live off vegetation they have harvested, dried and stored. Apparently, the calls that announce your presence are not warnings to fellow conies—or pikas and rock rabbits, as they are also called—but assertions of their territorial rights. The faint use path that heads right where the main trail crosses over the ridge crest passes three viewpoints that afford extensive views up and down the Gorge. The route once looped back and rejoined the main trail east of the rock swath but this eastern end is now almost indiscernible. Begin descending and switch back at the junction of the section of the Gorge Trail No. 400 that connects with the Multnomah Creek Trail (No's. 7 through 10). Note the ruins of a rock wall upslope from this turn.

Descend to the east, staying on the main trail where a tread heads down to the left, and continue dropping to the Scenic Highway. Walk along the shoulder of the road for 0.2 mile to the lower end of Oneonta Gorge. Late in the summer, when the water level is at its lowest, many people thoroughly enjoy picking their ways along the stream bed beneath those overhanging walls to the base of Oneonta Falls. To reach your starting point, continue east along the Scenic Highway another 0.3 mile.

Oneonta Creek Gorge

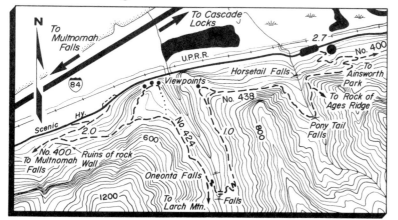

14 ROCK of AGES RIDGE

One day trip
Distance: 3 miles one way
Elevation gain: 2,700 feet
High point: 2,800 feet
Allow 2½ to 3 hours one way
Usually open late May through November
Topographic map:
  U.S.G.S. Bridal Veil, Wash.-Oreg.
  15'   1954

For steep, unremitting uphill the beginning portion of the use path along Rock of Ages Ridge, a route that connects the trail past Ponytail Falls (No. 13) and the Horsetail Creek Trail (No. 12) but never actually goes to Rock of Ages, is a first cousin to the use paths on Munra Point (No. 17) and Ruckel Ridge (No. 24). However, several short side paths lead to the precipitous edge of the ridge and impressive views up river so people whose spirits are stronger than their flesh have ample excuses for rest stops. Plus, once you get beyond aptly named Devils Backbone at 0.9 mile the grade and the tread become relatively more reasonable.

Usually, scrambling up these kinds of routes is more fun than coming down and the descent of the Rock of Ages Ridge route can be avoided by making one of two possible loops. Returning along the Horsetail Creek Trail takes you right back to your starting point and would be a total of 9.7 miles. Or you could establish a short car shuttle and return along the Nesmith Point Trail (No. 15), which would be total of 10.5 miles. Begin with adequate water.

Drive on the Scenic Highway 5.7 miles east of the junction of the road up from the Bridal Veil Exit 28 off I-84 (not accessible to west bound traffic) or 1.4 miles west from the Ainsworth Park Exit 35 to the large parking area at Horsetail Falls.

Climb to the east and continue up in five switchbacks. The Gorge Trail No. 400 heads east at the third turn. Beyond the final switchback walk west along the rock face and just as you curve into the canyon holding Ponytail Falls turn left and follow the unsigned path up the slope. Very quickly gain elevation and where you come to a three-way fork stay right to continue on the main trail and traverse. The route to the left contours to a viewpoint and the middle path climbs to another one. Come to a small open perch. A path to the left traverses for a few hundred feet and then winds steeply up for several yards to a natural arch of conglomerate on the rim of a sheer wall. The cliff faces and rock outcroppings you'll see as you look east show the many successive layers of lava that have created this section of the Gorge. Be warned that this lowest section of the Rock of Ages use path seems always to be changing, so you may find a few more junctions with paths heading off to the east.

The main route traverses an open slope and then re-enters woods before again rising very steeply. Farther on clamber up a rock section several yards high and beyond it stay left and traverse along the east side of Devils Backbone. Traverse up to the flat, open area at the upper end of the spiny formation that is an excellent spot for a snack stop. Not only does the crest here provide room enough to stretch out it also affords views of many landmarks in addition to those you've already seen, such as Mt. Adams, Hamilton (No. 2) and Table Mountains, Beacon Rock (No. 1), Bonneville Dam and St. Peters Dome.

Immediately south of Devils Backbone, re-enter woods and begin climbing along the crest on a much better tread and at a grade that still is generally steep but considerably easier than what you've just done. After about 0.6 mile come to a faint path on your left. A little side loop can be made by following this path to a T-junction near the cliff's edge. The route to the right climbs back up to the main trail and the one to the left follows along the crest to an exposed viewpoint on a rocky hump.

Drop slightly and then resume climbing steeply. Near 1.9 miles the crest broadens, the character of the woods changes and 0.5 mile farther the trail follows near the edge of the basin west of Yeon Mountain. Climb gradually near the rim for 0.6 mile to the junction of the Horsetail Creek Trail. Turn right to make the loop back to your starting spot or turn left to return along the Nesmith Trail.

Hikers on Devils Backbone

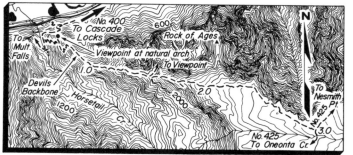

15 NESMITH POINT

One day trip
Distance: 5 miles one way
Elevation gain: 3,810 feet
High point: 3,872 feet
Allow 3½ to 4 hours one way
Usually open June through November
Topographic maps:
　U.S.G.S. Bridal Veil, Wash.-Oreg.
　15'　　　　　　　　　　1954
　U.S.G.S. Tanner Butte, Oreg.-Wash.
　7.5'　　　　　　　　　　1979

Between 1.0 and 3.0 miles the trail to Nesmith Point winds up through two immense, attractive basins unlike any others visited in the Gorge. Although the view from the former fire lookout site on Nesmith Point has been blocked for years now by big trees, the panorama right at the Gorge rim just before the summit is impressive and includes a bird's-eye view down onto Beacon Rock (No.1) and beyond to Hamilton (No. 2) and Table Mountains. A satisfying turnaround point for people who want a shorter hike is at the 3.0 mile point on the rim above the upper of those two spectacular basins. Note stopping here is just shorter, not all that much easier, because you will have climbed 2,800 feet. Shuttle fanciers can return along the Horsetail Creek Trail (No. 12).

From the west, drive on I-84 to the Ainsworth Park Exit 35. Turn left at the end of the exit, following the signs to Dodson and Warrendale, and then after 150 feet turn right onto Frontage Road—don't go back onto the freeway. Travel east on the frontage road 2.3 miles to the large parking area for Yeon State Park just before the road joins the eastbound lanes of the freeway. If you're approaching from the east, continue 2.7 miles west of the Bonneville Dam Exit 40 to

the Dodson-Warrendale Exit 37. After going under the freeway turn left and proceed 0.4 mile to the parking area.

Climb for several yards along the signed trail that begins at the northwestern side of the parking area, switch back and after 75 feet come to the junction of the Gorge Trail No. 400. The route that continues straight passes Elowah Falls (No. 16) after 0.8 mile. Turn right and meander up through woods. Cross a small side stream, traverse a slope of mossy talus and come to a junction above a wide, rocky stream bed that is dry much of the year. The Gorge Trail heads east across the bridge here and after 1.5 miles meets McLoughlin Parkway at Bonneville School.

Turn left—don't cross the bridge—and climb, with one set of short switchbacks, to the edge of the lower basin. Travel up its west wall, cross to the east side, go back to the west and wind up in short switchbacks. Traverse west out of the basin along a face and then climb in a second series of short switchbacks and enter a higher, bigger basin. Cross to its east side and eventually wind up in woods to the narrow crest of the top of the upper basin. The path to the left here connects with the trail to Upper Elowah Falls (refer to No. 23 in *50 Hiking Trails—Portland and Northwest Oregon* for a description of this abandoned route.)

To continue the hike to Nesmith Point, turn right at the crest. Traverse up the wooded slope for 0.4 mile and then veer right and continue traversing, but at a more gradual grade, along the southeast facing slope. Descend slightly, resume climbing and pass through two small, open areas. Come to a signed junction at 4.6 miles where the trail curves sharply right. If you are making the loop back along the Horsetail Creek Trail and want to save 0.4 mile and 400 feet of uphill, you can by-pass Nesmith Point by staying straight (left) here and following the faint trail for 0.1 mile to Road 222. The upper end of the Moffett Creek Trail, re-opened in 1980, is 0.6 mile down this road (refer to No. 24 in the *50 Hiking Trails — Portland and Northwest Oregon*). To reach the Horsetail Creek Trail, turn right at the road and walk up it for 200 yards to the sign marking Horsetail Creek Way No. 425 on your left.

To reach Nesmith Point, turn right at the junction at 4.6 miles and climb along the main trail for a short distance to Road 222. Turn right and wind up the road for 0.2 mile. Where you come near the rim curve right and follow a path for several yards to the rocky spot that once supported the lookout cabin.

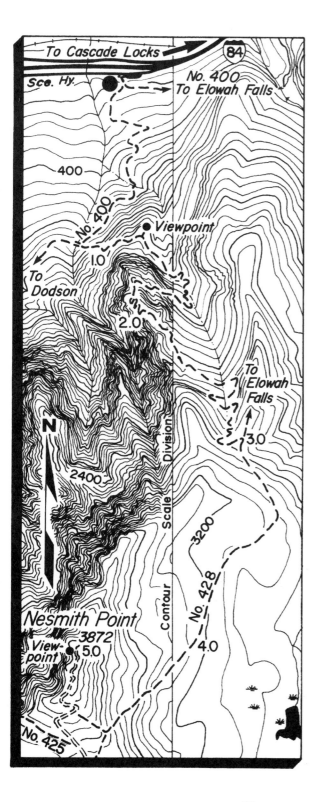

To Cascade Locks → 84

Sce. Hy.

No. 400
To Elowah Falls

400

No. 400

● Viewpoint

1.0

To
Dodson

2.0

To
Elowah
Falls

N

3.0

2400

Scale Division Contour

3200

No. 428

Nesmith Point

3872
5.0

View-
point

4.0

No. 425

16 ELOWAH FALLS TRAIL

One-half day trip
Distance: 1 mile to Upper Elowah Falls;
        0.8 mile to Lower Elowah Falls
Elevation gain: 425 feet to Upper Elowah
        Falls; 200 feet to Lower
        Elowah Falls; loss 100 feet
High point: 500 feet
Allow ½ hour to Upper Elowah Falls
Usually open February through December
Topographic maps:
  U.S.G.S. Bridal Veil, Wash.-Oreg.
  15'   1954
  U.S.G.S. Tanner Butte, Oreg.-Wash.
  7.5'   1979

The short, two pronged trail to Upper and Lower Elowah Falls is among the *creme de la creme* of Gorge hikes. A portion of the higher route traverses a section that has been cut out of a 300 foot high, sheer rock wall and then continues several hundred yards beyond the view of the upper falls to a level spot beside McCord Creek. The other fork follows the floor of a deep, narrow canyon to the base of the lower cascade, one of the most attractive in the Gorge.

From the west, proceed on I-84 to the Ainsworth Park Exit 35. Turn left at the end of the exit, following the signs to Dodson and Warrendale, and then after 150 feet keep right on the signed Frontage Road—don't go back onto the freeway. Travel east on the frontage road for 2.3 miles to a large parking area at Yeon State Park just before the road joins the eastbound lanes of the freeway. If you're approaching from the east, take the Dodson-Warrendale Exit 37, which is 2.7 miles west of the Bonneville Dam Exit 40. After going under the freeway turn left and drive 0.4 mile to the parking area. The signed trail begins from its northwestern side.

After several yards switch back left near an old water tank and 75 feet farther keep straight (left) at the junction of the route to Nesmith Point (No. 15) and the section of the Gorge Trail 400 that heads west to Bonneville School. Walk through a corridor of deciduous growth and then climb in an elegant woods of widely spaced conifers to the possibly unsigned junction of the upper and lower trails.

To follow the higher route, turn right and travel along a mostly open slope, switch back past particularly robust poison oak and then traverse through woods to the edge of the side canyon holding McCord Creek. Switch back and just before the next turn cross a large, old rusted water diversion pipe. Make two more short switchbacks and come to the edge of the precipitous canyon. Sturdy new metal railings now offer reassurance on the exposed side of the traverse along the wall but before the renaissance of trail rebuilding in the Gorge from the late 60's through the 70's negotiating this section always increased hikers' adrenalin output. From this aerie you can see Mt. Adams and Table Mountain in Washington and a section of the Columbia River.

Beyond the cliff face re-enter woods and pass the upper falls, which usually plunges in multiple streamers unlike the lower one that catapults over the edge in a single, long cascade. The trail continues on the level for a short distance and then stops where it comes to the bank of McCord Creek. The stream has had several designations, including Pierce and Kelly, but ultimately was named for a pioneer settler who built the first fish wheels near its mouth. The use path heading upslope just before the stream is the route of an old trail that connects with the Nesmith Point Trail (refer to No. 23 in *50 Hiking Trails—Portland and Northwest Oregon* for a detailed description of this route).

To reach the base of the lower falls, contour east from the junction at 0.3 miles. Cross a rocky slope and curve into McCord Creek canyon. Descend in six short switchbacks and then walk to near the head of the defile and the base of the 289 foot high falls.

The first trail to both falls began on the east side of the creek from the original Columbia River Highway but construction of the freeway destroyed this initial section of tread. Nature also did her bit to obliterate the first trail by sending down a former viewpoint, the immense boulder now snuggled against the route just above the east side of the creek. You can locate a section of that original trail by continuing along the Gorge Trail 400 a short distance beyond the boulder to an unsigned, overgrown path heading off to the right. No. 400 continues east past the route up Munra Point (No. 17) to the Bonneville interchange.

40

Elowah Falls

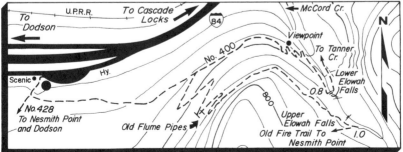

17 MUNRA POINT

One-half day trip
Distance: 2.5 miles one way
Elevation gain: 1,900 feet; loss 150 feet
High point: 1,860 feet
Allow 2 hours one way
Usually open March through December
Topographic maps:
 U.S.G.S. Bonneville Dam, Wash.-Oreg.
 7.5'   1979
 U.S.G.S. Tanner Butte, Oreg.-Wash.
 7.5'   1979

Munra Point is the most northerly of the several knobby rock outcroppings on the crest of the open, narrow ridge just west of Bonneville Dam and the relatively short climb to its summit involves some of the steepest uphill in the Gorge. Fortunately for people who prefer to warm-up before such a workout, the first half of the hike follows the typically gentle grade of the Gorge Trail No. 400. This hike is best saved for a warm, sunny day after a dry spell. The crest, though not commodious, still is a fine place to enjoy a leisurely lunch and the panorama, which includes the Columbia River, Mt. Adams, the tip of Mt. Rainier, Beacon Rock (No. 1), Hamilton (No. 2) and Table Mountains, Bonneville Dam, the Bridge of the Gods and the town of Stevenson. Secondly, the steep sections of the climb are considerably less fun when they're wet. People who want a longer hike can continue south along the open ridge for 0.2 mile and then follow an abandoned trail through woods for about 1.0 mile before the tread becomes faint. According to old maps, this route ended at a road near BPA power lines. No water is available along the hike.

Drive on I-84 to the Bonneville Dam Exit 40. If you're approaching from the west turn right at the end of the exit or, if you're coming from the east, turn left and go under the freeway. After 75 feet come to a fork and park in the area off to the right. The road to the south here goes to the start of the Tanner Creek Falls Trail (No. 18) and the road up to the left eventually passes the

start of the hikes No's. 19, 20 and 21.

Go around the gate, pass a sign stating Gorge Trail 400 and cross Tanner Creek on one of the original Columbia River Highway bridges. After about 200 feet stay straight (right) where another road heads down toward the stream, 100 feet farther curve up to the left and begin climbing along a trail. Switch back and curve around to the north facing slope. Traverse to an old road and follow along it at a slightly downhill grade, pass near a gate between you and I-84 and continue west on the vegetation clogged road to the resumption of a trail proper. Eventually, cross the bottom end of a small rocky area and farther on begin gradually descending. After about 0.2 mile of downhill be watching for an obvious, but unsigned, trail on your left. The Gorge Trail continues west, crosses Moffett Creek in 0.1 mile and continues another 1.3 miles to McCord Creek (No. 16).

Turn left and initially follow an excellent tread. Begin rising more steeply and then come to a messy section that involves only a few yards of scrambling. A short distance farther make two tidy switchbacks and traverse to a gully. Turn up it and after 75 feet stay right—do not continue up the gully—and follow the rubbly tread up to the crest of the ridge. The section from the bottom of the gully to the crest is the only portion of the hike that verges on not being fun, both going up and descending. Although not dense, poison oak is scattered about so be careful where you put your hands.

Turn right at the crest and follow the use path up the narrow ridge top, traveling mostly in the open but occasionally through woodsy patches. Of the two rock outcroppings you clamber up the higher one can be circumvented on its south side on the way back and the lower one is no problem to hike directly down. Farther along one of the forested sections come to a rock pitch about seven feet high and easily climb it.

At 1.9 miles curve left, briefly traverse and be watching for an ill-defined switchback to the right. Curve around to the steep, mostly grassy west facing slope, traverse at a gradual, mostly uphill grade across it and then make one final, short climb to the crest of Munra Ridge, named for "Grandma Munra", who for many years operated a railroad restaurant at Bonneville Dam. To see more landmarks turn left and head north along the crest. At a fork one spur climbs to the summit of Munra Point and the other contours along the west slope to another viewpoint. A narrow, exposed path traverses north from here to an overlook above Bonneville Dam.

Munra Point and Table Mountain

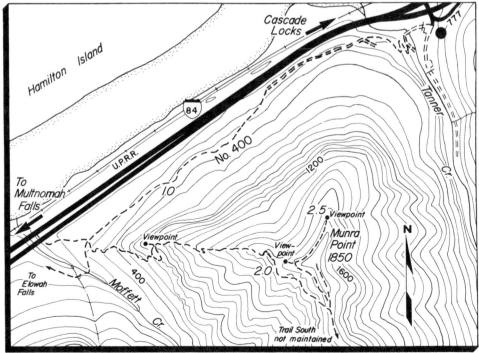

18 TANNER CREEK FALLS TRAIL

One-half day trip
Distance: 0.9 mile one way
Elevation gain: 340 feet; loss 100 feet
High point: 380 feet
Allow ½ hour one way
Usually open February through December
Topographic maps:
  U.S.G.S. Bonneville Dam, Wash.-Oreg.
  7.5'   **1979**
  U.S.G.S. Tanner Butte, Oreg.-Wash.
  7.5'   **1979**

The traverse along the east wall of lower Tanner Creek canyon to the glade of cedar trees at the base of Tanner Creek Falls, which is on most people's A List of scenic Gorge cascades, always has been a charming hike in spite of the rustic condition of the trail. But in 1987 volunteers under Forest Service supervision not only rerouted and upgraded the worst stretches of tread, they also constructed a new trail along a section of the west wall. So now the upper part of the hike can be done as a loop. Note that, as of early 1988, the two bridges that will connect both ends of this circuit were not in place but they are expected to be installed by late spring of that year.

Proceed on I-84 to the Bonneville Dam Exit 40. If you're approaching from the west turn right at the end of the exit or, if you're coming from the east, turn left and go under the freeway. After 75 feet come to a T-junction and park in the area off to the right. The road up to the left goes to the trailheads for hikes No's. 19, 20 and 21 and the signed Gorge Trail No. 400 crosses the ruins of one of the original Columbia River Highway bridges and continues west, passing the Munra Point Trail (No. 17) after 1.3 miles. The section of the Gorge Trail that heads southeast from the T-junction climbs to the Tanner Road and then continues below Wauna Viewpoint (No. 22) to Eagle Creek.

Walk along the road that parallels the east side of Tanner Creek, named for a man who had a donation land claim near the mouth of the stream, and after 200 yards go around a gate. You can see a couple of sections of the old flume for the Bonneville fish hatchery above to the left. Just before the end of the road pass a fence that encloses the modern intake apparatus for the hatchery. Several yards beyond where the trail proper begins cross directly below a waterfall. A bridge will be installed here at the same time as the ones on the loop. Interestingly, all three spans are scheduled to be brought in by helicopter.

Where the trail forks after a short distance take the higher (left) route. Farther on climb 36 steps with railroad ties for risers. Turn around for a view of Table Mountain on the Washington side and if you look up to the west you can see a portion of the open, rocky area that comprises the summit of Munra Ridge, which forms the west wall of Tanner Creek canyon. Walk on the level and then drop to the lower end of the loop. The trail to the right continues down in one set of short switchbacks to Tanner Creek.

It doesn't really matter which branch you take at the fork but if you opt to make the circuit in a clockwise direction stay left and traverse. In a short distance you'll be able to see down onto the western portion of the loop. The massive slide that it crosses occurred in 1973 and damned the creek long enough to cause consternation at the Bonneville fish hatchery because those fingerlings need a constant supply of fresh water. Fortunately, the flow resumed soon enough to prevent damage. Although less intimidating than when it was brand new, the slide still is a classic example of the innate instability of the Earth's surface. Begin gently descending and then curve down to the flat area near the pool at the base of the cascade, once named Wahclella Falls. You'll most likely want to spend some time here savoring the scene.

Tanner Creek Falls

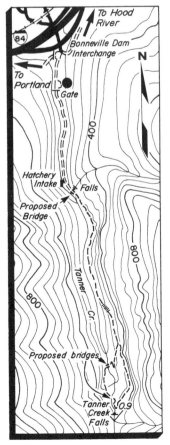

19 TANNER CUTOFF TRAIL to DUBLIN LAKE

One day trip or backpack
Distance: 4.9 miles to Dublin Lake
Elevation gain: 2,700 feet; loss 700 feet
High point: 3,700 feet
Allow 3 to 3½ hours one way
Usually open mid May through November
Topographic maps:
    U.S.G.S. Bonneville Dam, Wash.-Oreg.
    7.5'   **1979**
    U.S.G.S. Tanner Butte, Oreg.-Wash.
    7.5'   **1979**

That the Tanner Cutoff Trail, which connects the Tanner Creek Trail with the route along the crest of Tanner Ridge, is nicknamed the Billy Goat Trail should give a clue to the steepness of this route that gains 2,500 feet of elevation in just two miles. However, the first 2.0 miles of the hike is along a road and the steep descent can be avoided by returning along the moderately graded Tanner Butte Trail (No. 21), a highly recommended loop that would add no mileage and actually save 400 feet of uphill.

Drive on I-84 to the Bonneville Dam Exit 40. If you're approaching from the west turn right at the end of the exit or, if you're coming from the east, turn left and go under the freeway. After 75 feet come to a T-junction. Hikes No's. 17 and 18 begin to the right. Turn left, following the sign to Tanner Butte Trail, and traverse up to the east. After 0.3 mile curve sharply right and follow Road 777 for 2.1 miles to the head of a little canyon and the signed beginning of the Tanner Butte Trail. If you're intending to make the suggested loop, you could park here and then at the end of the hike you wouldn't have to walk up the road to the start of the Tanner Cutoff Trail. Continue along the road, on foot or in your car, for another 0.6 mile to a gate and a big sign stating Tanner Creek Trail No. 431, 3 miles. This gate is supposed to be closed, although you may find it open because vandals keep breaking the locks.

Walk along the road, which is not a dreary task at all because the slope is so lushly vegetated and the occasional views include Munra Point and a good portion of the Tanner Creek drainage. About 1.0 mile from the gate begin descending and 0.9 mile farther come to a wide spot in the road and a bevy of trail signs on the right pointing across the bed. If the policy changes and it's legal to drive to this point, DO NOT CONTINUE beyond the start of the trail proper because the road becomes very steep and rough.

Turn left from the road onto the trail and walk through woods thick with big leaf maples, passing a marker identifying the boundary of the Columbia Wilderness after a few hundred yards. One hundred feet beyond it cross a stream and a few hundred feet farther come to the junction of the Tanner Cutoff Trail. The Tanner Creek Trail continues parallel to its namesake for about one mile and then peters out. However, heading west just before its end is the demanding Moffett Creek Trail (No. 24 in *50 Hiking Trails — Portland and Northwest Oregon*) that climbs for about 5.8 miles to Nesmith Point (No. 15).

Turn left, start climbing, initially at a reasonable enough grade, and eventually cross a stream, the last source of water. Not far beyond it travel near the base of a scree slope and begin switch backing. At the sixteenth turn the grade increases from steep to very steep. Two switchbacks and a long traverse farther come to the north facing slope. Stay on it for just a few yards and then curve right and begin winding up the nose of the ridge for 0.7 mile at that same very steep grade. As it does throughout the Gorge, the first appearance of beargrass, on this specific hike around the 4.0 mile point, indicates the end of the uphill is near. Sure enough, not much farther begin climbing at an increasingly gentle grade that is almost level by the time you come to the crest and the Tanner Butte Trail.

To reach Dublin Lake, turn right and follow the crest for 150 yards to the signed spur. Turn left, walk on the level for 100 feet, drop moderately for another 100 feet and then descend steeply for several hundred yards, losing a total of 250 feet of elevation, to the northwest end of the lake, which occupies the floor of a wooded bench.

To make the recommended loop, follow the Tanner Butte Trail down along the crest, stay left at the junction of the route to Wauna Point (No. 20), and continue down. Cross a power line access road and descend for the final 0.3 mile to Road 777.

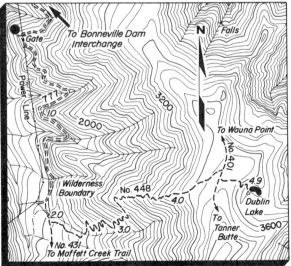

20 WAUNA POINT

One day trip
Distance: 3 miles one way
Elevation gain: 1,550 feet; loss 650 feet
High point: 2,650 feet
Allow 2½ hours one way
Usually open April through November
Topographic maps:
    U.S.G.S. Bonneville Dam, Wash.-Oreg.
    7.5'   1959
    U.S.G.S. Tanner Butte, Oreg.-Wash.
    7.5'   1959

The actual Wauna Point is a knoll in deep woods but a rustic path winds down from the forested knob to an open, aerie perch 2,000 feet above Bonneville Dam. This is one of those places where you'll want to spend considerable time observing traffic through the locks, the construction of the new locks and the trains along the river's edge. Natural features you can enjoy include Ruckel Ridge (No. 24) directly to the east across Eagle Creek canyon, west to equally precipitous Munra Point (No. 17) and north to Beacon Rock (No. 1), Table and Hamilton (No. 2) Mountains and Mt. Adams.

The final 0.3 mile of the hike is along a sometimes exposed tread that is more fun than difficult to negotiate. Only inexperienced hikers or people with vertigo would have any problems. Energetic types who want a longer outing can make a 9.5 mile loop by returning along Trail No. 448, which leaves the Tanner Butte Trail 2.0 miles south of its junction with the spur to Wauna Point and then follows Tanner Road back to the starting point (refer to No. 19).

Drive on I-84 to the Bonneville Dam Exit 40. Approaching from the west, turn right at the end of the exit or coming from the east, turn left and go under the freeway. After 75 feet come to a T-junction. Hikes No's. 17 and 18 begin to the right. Turn left, following the sign to Tanner Butte Trail, and traverse up to the east. After 0.3 mile curve sharply right and follow Road 777 for 2.1 miles to the head of a little canyon and the beginning of the Tanner Butte Trail No. 401.

Walk on the level for 150 feet and then wind up in a set of short switchbacks. Cross a small stream, curve into a larger side canyon and traverse to a second creek, the last dependable source of water. Head out of the canyon and then travel along the face of a cleared slope where you'll be able to see pyramid shaped Mt. Talapus in the Bull Run Reserve and have the first views of Munra Point and Hamilton and Table Mountains.

Cross the power line access road, re-enter woods and begin a steady climb. Switch back left, traverse and switch back right at the nose of a ridge. Return to that crest twice more, crossing briefly to the east side both times, and then make six switchbacks up the face of the slope, coming to a short spur to a rocky viewpoint at the last turn. Have a long traverse along the wall of a basin, pass a small spring that may not flow all year and 0.1 mile farther come to the signed junction of the spur to Wauna Point.

Turn left and walk gradually downhill through woods for 0.2 mile to a sign stating Wauna Point 300 feet. Of course, you can follow this route if you're curious, but you won't see much.

To reach the recommended overlook, turn left near the sign and descend to the west for a short distance. Curve sharply right several yards east of a small spring and traverse on a narrow tread. Wind down in a series of very short and steep switchbacks to a narrow crest. Walk along the ridge top to a big hump, stay left and traverse up along its west slope. Pick your way down a narrow rock rib for 100 yards to the open, flat overlook and those promised views.

Falls at start of Tanner Butte Trail

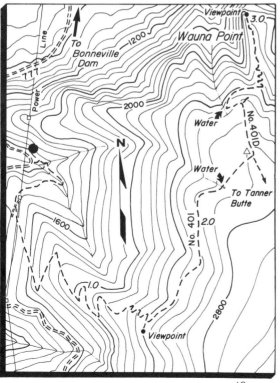

21 TANNER BUTTE

One day trip
Distance: 8 miles one way
Elevation gain: 3,650 feet; loss 150 feet
High point: 4,500 feet
Allow 4 to 5 hours one way
Usually open mid June through November
Topographic map:
U.S.G.S. Tanner Butte, Oreg.-Wash.
7.5'   1979

The awesome view from the rocky top of massive Tanner Butte encompasses an astounding collection of landmarks between Mt. Jefferson and Mt. Rainier. Absolutely make this hike on a clear day and plan to spend a lot of time on the summit oohing and aahing over the panorama and identifying geographic features. If you do the trip during late August also allow extra time for harvesting some of the huckleberries that abundantly line the old roadbed between 5.5 and 7.5 miles. Although this is a long, hard hike, the grade is moderate to gentle, except for the final 0.3 mile, which is mostly a steep bushwhack. You can make a loop trip, which would add no extra mileage, by returning along Trail No. 448 (No. 19).

Drive on I-84 to the Bonneville Dam Exit 40. Approaching from the west, turn right at the end of the exit or coming from the east, turn left and go under the freeway. After 75 feet come to a T-junction. Hike No's. 17 and 18 begin to the right. Turn left, following the sign to Tanner Butte Trail, and traverse up to the east. After 0.3 mile curve sharply right and follow Road 777 for 2.1 miles to the head of a little canyon and the signed trailhead.

Walk on the level for 150 feet and then wind up in a set of short switchbacks. Cross a small stream, curve into a larger side canyon and cross a second creek, the last dependable source of water. Traverse out of the canyon and travel along the face of a cleared slope where you'll be able to see pyramid shaped Mt. Talapus in the Bull Run Reserve, Munra Point (No. 17) and Hamilton (No. 2) and Table Mountains on the Washington side of the Gorge.

Cross the power line access road, re-enter woods and begin a steady climb. Switch back left, traverse and switch back right at the nose of the ridge. Return to that crest twice, crossing briefly to the east side each time, and then make six switchbacks up the face of the slope, coming at the last to a short spur to a rocky viewpoint that affords sightings west to Munra, Wauneka and Nesmith Ridges. Have a long traverse on the wall of a basin, pass a small spring that may not flow all year and 0.1 mile farther come to the junction of the spur to Wauna Point (No. 20).

Stay right and head up along the broad, wooded crest, passing the marker identifying the boundary of the Columbia Wilderness after 0.3 mile. Continue moderately uphill to the signed junction of Trail No. 448. Stay straight and 150 yards farther come to the signed spur that drops for 0.3 mile and loses 250 feet of elevation to Dublin Lake. Keep straight (right) and in 0.2 mile come to an overgrown road.

Turn left and follow the gently graded old bed along the west side of the forested slope. Eventually, walk through a more open area, re-enter woods and begin gradually descending. Have your first view ahead to Tanner Butte and beyond to Mt. Hood and go around the west side of a big hump. Cross a long, treeless saddle and resume climbing along the road. About 0.4 mile from the saddle be watching for a sign above on your left that marks the start of the "Scramble Route" to Tanner Butte. You can follow this faint tread that eventually becomes nonexistent but an easier (as in considerably less vegetated) way is to continue along the road for another 0.1 mile and take an unsigned path. Unlike the "Scramble Route", this more southeasterly approach becomes better defined the higher you climb.

A partial listing of what you can see from the former lookout site on the summit includes Mt. Jefferson, Olallie Butte, Bull of the Woods, Saddle Mountain in the Coast Range, Mt. Hood, and, in Washington, Mounts Adams, Rainier and St. Helens, the Goat Rocks, Silver Star and Grassy Knoll. A few of the landmarks on the Oregon side of the Gorge are Larch Mountain (No's. 9, 10 and 11), Nesmith Point (No. 15), the Benson Plateau and Chinidere Mountain (No. 26) and Mt. Defiance (No. 33).

Looking east from Tanner Ridge

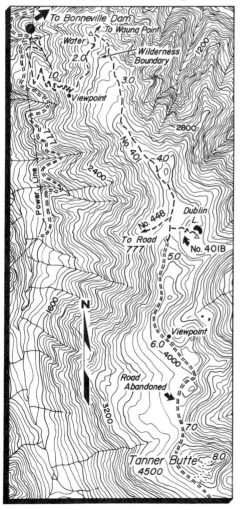

22 WAUNA VIEWPOINT

One-half day trip
Distance: 1.8 miles one way
Elevation gain: 800 feet
High point: 940 feet
Allow 1 hour one way
Usually open February through December
Topographic maps:
    U.S.G.S. Bonneville Dam, Wash.-Oreg.
    7.5'   **1979**
    U.S.G.S. Tanner Butte, Oreg.-Wash
    7.5'   **1979**

Wauna Viewpoint is a small level spot about one-third of the way up Wauna Point (No. 20) proper but the panorama from the less lofty perch certainly is not one-third as impressive. Tanner Ridge forms the west wall of Eagle Creek canyon and the view east across this gorge includes nearby Ruckel Ridge (No. 24) and the slopes traversed by the Ruckel Creek Trail (No. 25). In addition to landmarks on the Washington side of the Gorge, such as Hamilton (No. 2) and Table Mountains, the view north includes Mt. Adams. But probably the most intriguing feature is Bonneville Dam and Locks directly below. And making a special one time appearance through the early 1990's is the construction of a new ship lock.

Approaching from the west proceed on I-84 to the Eagle Creek Park Exit 41. Turn right at the end of the exit, in 200 feet come to a fork and stay straight (right), as if you were going to the Eagle Creek trailhead (No. 23). After 50 yards come to spaces for parking on your left below a portion of the picnic area. After the hike you'll need to drive east on the freeway 1.4 miles to the Cascade Locks Exit 44. If you're approaching from the east, take the Bonneville Dam Exit 40 and then head east 1.2 miles to the Eagle Creek Park exit.

Walk east along the road from the parking area for several yards to the large suspension bridge over Eagle Creek. At the other end of the span turn right or left and follow either leg of the signed Nature Trail Loop. On the return, you can take the section you didn't follow on the way up.

From the top end of the loop continue climbing and then switch back and traverse above the fish hatchery. Curve around the face of the slope to a view of Bonneville Dam. Switch back from the overlook and after a short distance switch back again. Keep climbing along the wooded slope and then make one more set of turns and resume traversing to the junction of the spur up to Wauna Viewpoint. The Gorge Trail No. 400, the low level route that extends from Angels Rest (No. 5) east to Wyeth—or will when the final segment between Herman Camp (No. 30) and Wyeth (No. 31) is completed—continues for 0.5 mile to Tanner Road, follows it west for 0.2 mile and then heads down to the Bonneville Dam interchange. Tanner Road eventually passes the trailheads of hikes No's. 19, 20 and 21.

Turn left onto the trail to Wauna Viewpoint, traverse and then switch back five times. Cross a cleared area beneath the power lines, make one final turn and recross the open slope to the flat overlook under the tower. The concrete structure on the viewpoint was erected as a survey marker to aid in the construction of the new powerhouse at Bonneville Dam.

Ruckel Ridge from Wauna Viewpoint

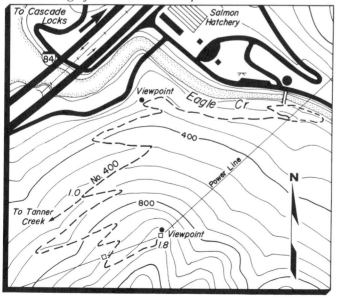

23 EAGLE CREEK TRAIL to WAHTUM LAKE

One day trip or backpack
Distance: 13 miles one way
Elevation gain: 3,750 feet
High point: 3,750 feet
Allow 8 to 10 hours one way
Usually open June through November
Topographic maps:
  U.S.G.S. Bonneville Dam, Wash.-Oreg.
  7.5'   1979
  U.S.G.S. Tanner Butte, Oreg.-Wash.
  7.5'   1979
  U.S.G.S. Wahtum Lake, Oreg.
  7.5'   1979

What with its moderate grade, sheer rock walls and many waterfalls the hike along the Eagle Creek Trail as far as the Punch Bowl at 2.1 miles justifiably is one of the most heavily used routes in the Gorge. Although less frequented beyond the Punch Bowl, the easy grade and spectacular scenery, which includes a long narrow chasm spanned by High Bridge and a tunnel carved behind a falls, continues for another 4.0 miles.

Energetic hikers can make a fun loop by taking the steep, Eagle-Benson Way Trail No. 434 from the 5.0 mile point up to the Benson Plateau (No. 26) and then returning along the Ruckel Creek Trail (No. 25), a circuit that would involve 15.2 miles with 4,200 feet of uphill. Backpackers can return to their starting point by taking the Ruckel Creek Trail down from the Benson Plateau or, using a car shuttle, they can loop back from Wahtum Lake along the Pacific Crest Trail (No. 26) or the Herman Creek Trail (No. 27). A Forest Service road reaches Wahtum Lake from the south but setting-up a car shuttle would involve a long drive through either Hood River or over Lolo Pass.

Camping before the 7.5 mile point is allowed at only four sites: Tenas, Wy'east, Blue Grouse and 7½ Mile Camps. As is true with most areas, backpackers should use portable stoves, not build wood fires.

From the west drive on I-84 to the Eagle Creek Park Exit 41, turn right at the end of the exit and after 200 feet come to a fork just before a stone rest room building. Keep right and continue 0.6 mile, passing the start of hike No. 22, to the road's end. To return westbound after the hike, continue 1.4 miles east on I-84 to the Cascade Locks Exit 44. Approaching from the east, take I-84 to the Bonneville Dam Exit 40 and then head east 1.2 miles.

Traverse the wooded slope along a trail that is paved for the first 0.3 mile and after 0.7 mile travel along a sheer rock wall several hundred feet above Eagle Creek. Continue along somewhat less precipitous slopes, traveling through woods and occasional small grassy patches. At 1.5 miles a short side loop descends to a view of Metlako Falls. Ford Sorenson Creek, traverse out of its canyon and pass a sign identifying the 0.2 mile spur down to a rocky beach at stream level just below the Punch Bowl. A short distance farther the main trail comes to an overlook 100 feet above the Punch Bowl.

Cross Tish Creek and an unnamed side stream on bridges, at 3.0 miles begin walking above that narrow gorge and cross it on High Bridge. After 0.7 mile come to another span across Eagle Creek and continue traversing through woods. Enter the Columbia Wilderness and pass the signed lower end of the Eagle-Benson Way Trail. Traverse a scree slope and at 6.0 miles travel in and out of the canyon holding Tunnel Falls. Travel unnervingly close to the top of a falls and then walk beside the stream. If you're making a one day hike, the rocky bank between the trail and the flow here is a good place for a snack stop before heading back.

The main trail continues parallel to Eagle Creek, crosses two side streams and at 7.6 miles comes to the junction of the demanding, seldom taken Eagle-Tanner Trail to Tanner Butte. Turn sharply left and begin climbing through woods. Recross the two streams you forded before the switchback and at 9.3 miles come to Inspiration Point with its fine view over lower Eagle Creek gorge. Traverse up through deep woods, after 0.5 mile stay straight (left) at the junction of Trail No. 435 up to Indian Springs and continue climbing to Trail No. 445 on your left. It crosses the outlet of Wahtum Lake and meets the PCT near the junction of the spur up to Chinidere Mountain.

Keep straight (right) on Trail No. 440 and in 0.2 mile meet the PCT. The section to the right climbs to Indian Springs and continues south. Keep straight, continuing to parallel the shoreline. Campsites are scheduled to be relocated to the upslope side of the trail and also on the north side of the lake. The PCT curves around the east and north sides of the lake and eventually heads north along the Benson Plateau.

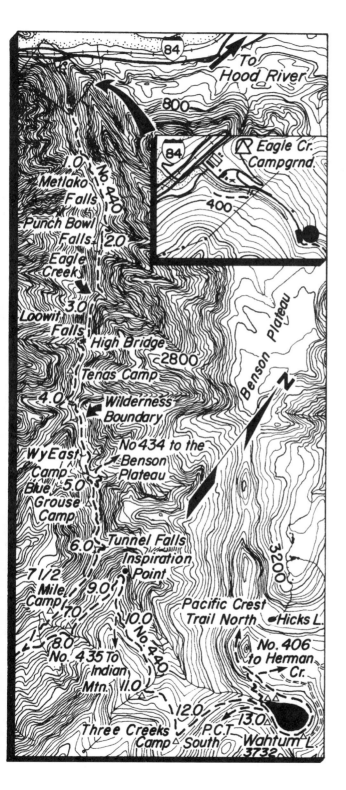

To
Hood River

84

800

84

Eagle Cr.
Campgrnd.

400

1.0

Metlako
Falls

No. 440

Punch Bowl
Falls 2.0

Eagle
Creek

3.0

Loowit
Falls

High Bridge
2800

Tenas Camp

4.0

Wilderness
Boundary

Benson Plateau

N

No. 434 to the
Benson
Plateau

Wy East
Camp
Blue 5.0
Grouse
Camp

3200

6.0 Tunnel Falls

Inspiration
Point

7 1/2
Mile 9.0
Camp
7.0

10.0

No. 440

Pacific Crest
Trail North   Hicks L.

8.0

No. 435 To
Indian
Mtn. 11.0

No. 406
to Herman
Cr.

12.0 13.0

Three Creeks
Camp   P.C.T.
South   Wahtum L.
3732

24 RUCKEL RIDGE

One day trip
Distance: 3.8 miles one way
Elevation gain: 3,700 feet; loss 100 feet
High point: 3,700 feet
Allow 3 hours one way
Usually open early May through November
Topographic maps:
  U.S.G.S. Bonneville Dam, Wash.-Oreg.
  7.5'   1979
  U.S.G.S. Carson, Wash.-Oreg.
  7.5'   1979

Although Ruckel Ridge, which forms the east wall of lower Eagle Creek canyon, is a favorite conditioning hike of mountaineers, the climb is an outstandingly interesting trip for anyone who enjoys steep grades and doesn't mind an occasional bit of exposure. If you plan to follow Ruckel Ridge for its entire length to the Benson Plateau, you're encouraged to return along the Ruckel Creek Trail (No. 25), one of the most spectacular routes in the Gorge, particularly in late April when the flower gardens in the Hanging Meadows are blooming. Carry water as none is available until 3.8 miles.

From the west proceed on I-84 to the Eagle Creek Park Exit 41. Turn right at the end of the exit, drive 200 feet to a parking area where the road forks and leave your car here in front of the stone rest room building. To return westbound after the hike, drive 1.4 miles east to the Cascade Locks exit. Approachng from the east, take I-84 to the Bonneville Dam Exit 40 and head east 1.2 miles to the Eagle Creek Park exit.

Walk northeast up the paved road to the campround for 75 yards to a sign on the left shoulder identifying the Gorge Trail No. 400. Wind up to the edge of a bluff above the freeway, turn right and follow along the fence to the north end of the campground and the junction of the route to Ruckel Creek Trail. Turn right, following the sign to Buck Point, and walk to a board fence. After several yards veer right onto a path

that goes past Campsite 11. Turn right at its access and then in several yards turn left at Campsite 10 onto another spur road and follow it up to the big sign between Campsites 5 and 6 identifying the Buck Point Trail. From here, the mileage to Buck Point actually is about .4 mile rather than the .75 mile shown on the marker.

After several yards turn right and climb moderately in six switchbacks. Traverse from the final turn for a few hundred feet to an obvious, but unsigned, fork at two large rocks and stay left. The branch to the right at the fork ends in 100 yards at Buck Point.

Wind up in six short switchbacks to a viewpoint at a cleared swath under a power line tower. Re-enter woods and then descend slightly before traversing a slope of lichen covered rocks. After a few hundred feet be watching for a switchback up to the left and follow it. Continue over small boulders and slabs in a northerly direction to the open, small, relatively flat crest at the north end of the ridge just above a line of trees. Turn right and walk southeast up the crest several yards to the bottom of the cliff face. Turn left and follow along the base of the wall and then curve right and begin climbing very steeply along the east side of the ridge. If you make the hike around mid April you'll periodically be face-to-face with perhaps the largest Calypso orchid blooms in the Gorge. Come to the narrow crest and follow the use path along it, alternating between wildflower splashed open areas and stretches in lush woods.

At 2.5 miles circumvent an extremely narrow section of rock outcroppings called the "Catwalk" by traversing below the crest on its south (right) side. Several hundred feet beyond where you rejoin the crest come to a large, open rocky hump. Curve right, traverse around its west and south sides, re-enter woods and drop slightly to a saddle. By here you're in the Columbia Wilderness.

Cross the saddle, follow the path up along the left side of the ridge and then climb steeply to the crest. Farther on it broadens and the trail winds up very steeply to the edge of the Benson Plateau where the grade abruptly levels off. Follow the faint tread and tree blazes in a northeasterly direction for 0.3 mile to Ruckel Creek. This level stretch also may be tagged. If you're making the loop, ford the stream and head gradually uphill to the northeast (left) at about a 30 degree angle to the stream until you intersect the Ruckel Creek Trail. Turn left and begin descending.

Hikers on Ruckel Ridge

25 RUCKEL CREEK TRAIL

One day trip
Distance: 4.6 miles one way
Elevation gain: 3,800 feet; loss 200 feet
High point: 3,700 feet
Allow 3 hours one way
Usually open early May through November
Topographic maps:
    U.S.G.S. Bonneville Dam, Wash.-Oreg.
    7.5'   1979
    U.S.G.S. Carson, Wash.-Oreg.
    7.5'   1979

During late April the huge hanging meadows traversed midway along the Ruckel Creek Trail support one of the most impressive wildflower displays in the Gorge. But even throughout the rest of the hiking season this moderately demanding route is an exceptionally varied and scenic trip that includes several viewpoints and a unique, large basin of lichen covered rocks. The trip can be done as a fun, but strenuous, loop by taking the Ruckel Ridge (No. 24) use path up and returning down the Ruckel Creek Trail.

From the west drive on I-84 to the Eagle Creek Park Exit 41, turn right at the end of the exit and drive 200 feet to a parking area where the road forks and leave your car here in front of the stone rest room building. To return west bound after the hike, continue 1.4 miles east on I-84 to the Cascade Locks Exit 44. Approaching from the east, take I-84 to the Bonneville Dam Exit 40 and then head east 1.2 miles to the Eagle Creek Park exit.

Walk northeast up the paved road to the campground for 75 yards to a sign on the left shoulder identifying the Gorge Trail No. 400. Wind up above the fish hatchery to the edge of a bluff above the freeway. Turn right and follow along the fence to the north end of the campground and the junction of the signed trail to Buck Point. Unless you're making the loop, keep left and descend to a large clearing. Follow the trail through the meadow to a section of the original Columbia River Highway and walk east along it for several hundred feet to Ruckel Creek.

At the east side of the ornate bridge over the stream turn right onto the Ruckel Creek Trail. The route of the Gorge Trail No. 400 continues along the Old Highway for 0.8 mile to the resumption of a trail. Parallel the flow for a short distance and then switch back left. At this turn you'll have the last easy access to a dependable water source until the very end of the hike. Climb in three more switchbacks to the cleared area around a power line tower. Ruckel Ridge, which deceptively appears to demand little effort to hike up, is directly to the south and visible during most of the climb. Switch back five more times to the edge of a large rocky bowl. At its far end resume traversing in woods, switch back twice and then wind up at a moderately steep grade on or near the crest of a narrow ridge.

Traverse, begin winding up and at the tenth turn pass a very exposed viewpoint where you can see Mounts Adams and St. Helens, the Bridge of the Gods and a long section of the Columbia River. Make two more sets of switchbacks and at a crest abruptly leave the coniferous woods and enter an area of grass and oaks. Curve left and traverse an open slope to a second, similarly vegetated crest where you'll have a particularly attractive perspective of Mt. Hood. Traverse two meadows separated by a finger of evergreens and continue at a gradual grade to the largest of the hanging meadows at 3.1 miles. There may be a small water source here through early summer.

At the east end of the open expanse resume traveling in woods and switch back four times. Traverse to a small, open slope and then begin climbing at a steep grade. Cross a rocky area and continue winding up through woods. By here you're in the Columbia Wilderness. Level off and soon pass the possibly unsigned junction on your left of the Rudolph Spur Trail that descends to the Gorge Trail No. 400, meeting it several yards west of the road that parallels Dry Creek. Taking the Rudolph Spur Trail up and returning along Ruckel Creek Trail is a superb loop for people who enjoy long, hard hikes (refer to No. 25 in *50 Hiking Trails—Portland and Northwest Oregon*). One hundred fifty yards farther along the main trail come to the possibly signed or tagged route right to Ruckel Ridge. If you want to have a snack stop at Ruckel Creek, angle downhill to the southwest for a few hundred yards. The main trail continues northeast another 1.3 miles to the Pacific Crest Trail and the east edge of the Benson Plateau (No. 26).

Hikers on upper portion of Ruckel Creek Trail

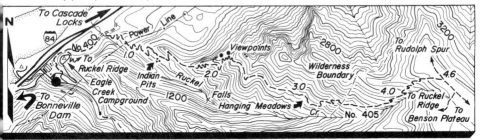

26 PACIFIC CREST TRAIL
to WAHTUM LAKE

One day trip or backpack
Distance: 13 miles one way
Elevation gain: 4,700 feet; loss 900 feet
High point: 4,300 feet
Allow 8 to 9 hours one way
Usually open June through November
Topographic maps:
   U.S.G.S. Carson, Wash.-Oreg.
   7.5' 1979
   U.S.G.S. Wahtum Lake, Oreg.
   7.5' 1979

After winding up to the rim of a 3,600 foot wall this hike travels along the eastern edge of the two mile long Benson Plateau and then follows a ridge to Wahtum Lake. Using a car shuttle, day hikers could make a loop by returning along the Ruckel Creek Trail (No. 25). Possible loops for backpackers include the Herman Creek Trail (No. 27) and, with a shuttle, the Eagle Creek Trail (No. 23). A Forest Service road reaches Wahtum Lake from the south but establishing a car shuttle would involve a long drive through either Hood River or over Lolo Pass. Take mosquito repellent and note that horses are permitted on this route. Beyond Teakettle Spring the PCT passes no easily accessible water sources until Wahtum Lake.

From the west proceed on I-84 to the Cascade Locks Exit 44. Drive about 1.0 mile through the community to its east end and turn left where a sign marks the road to Industrial Park and Airport. After 2.0 miles cross over the freeway, turn left and in 0.4 mile come to the Columbia Gorge Work Center. Approaching from the east, take the Forest Lane–Herman Creek exit between the 48 and 47 mileposts. After going under the freeway turn right and head west 0.6 mile.

If the paved road to the campground is open, follow it up to trailhead parking. However, if this road is blocked, turn right and drive to the northwest corner of the Work Center near the big green building. An obvious, through possibly unsigned, trail heads up from this alternate parking area and connects with the route from the campground.

Continue up from where the two trails join

and cross a narrow power line access road. Traverse, farther on make a set of short switchbacks and come to the junction of the trail to No's. 27 through 30. Stay right and descend slightly to an old road, soon resume traveling on a trail and drop to the bridge across Herman Creek. Wind up to the junction with the PCT, which begins (or ends) its northern Oregon portion at the Bridge of the Gods in Cascade Locks.

Turn left, cross a scree slope and re-enter woods. After two sets of switchbacks and a traverse wind up for 1.0 mile and then climb along a ridge crest to a helispot at 5.0 miles. Pass Teakettle Spring and continue up to the northeastern edge of the mostly level Benson Plateau. Between 6.3 and 8.5 miles continue on the PCT past four interconnecting routes that head west: the Benson Way No. 405B, which meets the Ruckel Creek Trail at Hunters Camp; the Benson-Ruckel Trail No. 405A; the Ruckel Creek Trail No. 405, which passes Benson Camp; and the southern end of No. 405B. Water is available off the PCT to the west at the two camps. Before you pass the last connector have the first superb view ahead to Mt. Hood and then begin descending. Beyond No. 405B continue down along the wooded east side of the ridge for 0.2 mile to Camp Smokey and the junction of the Eagle-Benson Trail No. 434 that connects with the Eagle Creek Trail (No. 23).

Continue in woods at an erratic, but always gentle, grade and at 9.5 miles contour along a large scree slope where you'll have views to the east. Cross to the other side of the ridge and traverse up through the remains of a burn that occurred in 1972.

Make one set of short switchbacks and 100 feet beyond the second turn pass a 75 foot long spur to a viewpoint. Continue uphill along the west side, passing the obscure junction of the long abandoned trail to Hicks Lake (see No. 28 in *50 Hiking Trails—Portland and Northwest Oregon*). Continue rising gradually through increasingly open terrain and then a few yards beyond where you re-enter woods come to the 0.3 mile spur to the summit of Chinidere Mountain. Stay straight on the PCT for 175 feet to the junction of Trail No. 445 that descends to the outlet of Wahtum Lake and the junction of the Eagle Creek Trail. To continue along the PCT to Wahtum Lake, keep straight and in several hundred feet meet the connector to the Herman Creek Trail. Stay right, descend and travel above the north and east shores. Beginning in 1988 new campsites are scheduled to be developed on the slopes above the lake.

Benson Plateau from the south

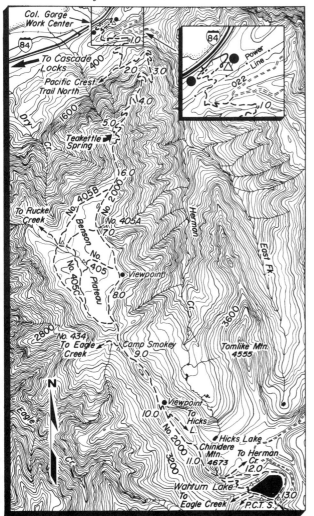

27 HERMAN CREEK TRAIL to WAHTUM LAKE

One day trip or backpack
Distance: 12.2 miles one way
Elevation gain: 3,900 feet; loss 350 feet
High point: 3,950 feet
Allow 6 to 7 hours one way
Usually open June through November
Topographic maps:
   U.S.G.S. Carson, Wash.-Oreg.
   7.5'   **1979**
   U.S.G.S. Wahtum Lake, Oreg.
   7.5'   **1979**

Because the Herman Creek Trail shares its starting point with three other routes (No's. 28, 29 and 30) and they all interconnect, several day loops are possible. Backpackers can make a perfect circuit by taking the Pacific Crest Trail back along the Benson Plateau (No. 26) or, by establishing a short car shuttle, returning on the Eagle Creek Trail (No. 23). A Forest Service road reaches Wahtum Lake from the south but establishing a car shuttle would involve a long drive through either Hood River or over Lolo Pass. Note that horses are allowed only on the Herman Creek and Pacific Crest Trails and the Herman Bridge Trail that connects the two.

From the west drive on I-84 to the Cascade Locks Exit 44. Proceed about 1.0 mile through the community to its east end and turn left where a sign marks the road to Industrial Park and Airport. After 2.0 miles cross over the freeway, turn left and head east 0.4 mile to the Columbia Gorge Work Center. Approaching from the east, take the Forest Lane-Herman Creek exit between the 48 and 47 mileposts. Go under the freeway, turn right and head west 0.6 mile to the Center. If the paved road to the campground is open, follow it up to trailhead parking. However, if it's blocked, turn right and drive to the northwest corner of the Work Center near the big green building. An obvious, though possibly unsigned, trail heads up from this alternate parking area and connects with the route from the campground.

Continue up from where the two trails join and cross a narrow power line access road. Traverse and after one set of short switchbacks come to the junction of the connector to the PCT. Turn left and after 200 yards come to a large, flat open area. Cross it in the same direction you were heading and then keep right where you meet a road. Climb along it, level off and at 1.4 miles pass the clearing at Herman Camp and the start of the Gorton Creek Trail (No. 30).

Continue along the road and after 300 yards pass the beginning of the Nick Eaton Trail (No. 29). The road narrows into the Herman Creek Trail after another 250 yards. Begin gradually dropping along the east wall of immense Herman Creek Canyon. Pass directly below two high waterfalls, travel uphill for a bit, traversing a more open slope of Oregon white oak along one section. Curve into a large side canyon, pass the Columbia Wilderness boundary marker, ford Camp Creek and traverse out the other side of the canyon. Have a bit more downhill to another waterfall before beginning an easy climb along a less precipitous slope and at 4.1 miles come to the junction of the Casey Creek Trail (No. 28) just before a campsite at a clearing. A spur descends from the west edge of the clearing for 0.4 mile to Herman Creek.

Stay straight and after a short level stretch begin climbing steadily. Along the next two miles make easy crossings of three large streams and five smaller ones. At 7.3 miles and just before the dilapidated Cedar Swamp shelter come to the junction of the Herman Creek Cutoff No. 410 to Green Point Mountain. Again keep straight (right), pass a water source a short distance beyond the shelter and farther on ford the East Fork of Herman Creek at 7.8 miles and pass 7½ Mile Camp.

Resume climbing along increasingly open slopes, switch back a few times and at 9.2 miles come to the junction of the 0.4 mile spur to Mud Lake. Keep right (straight), traverse a more open area and then switch back to the top of the ridge where a faint spur heads north for 1.0 mile with 500 feet of elevation gain to Tomlike Mountain. Stay left on the main trail and several yards farther come to the junction of the Anthill Trail that climbs for 0.5 mile to Road 1310. To reach Wahtum Lake, stay right on Trail 406 and walk through an area dense with glacier lilies early in the season. Stay right where you meet an old trail alignment and come to the PCT. To reach Wahtum Lake turn left and descend. (Refer to No. 26 for details on the immediate Wahtum Lake area.)

Wahtum Lake

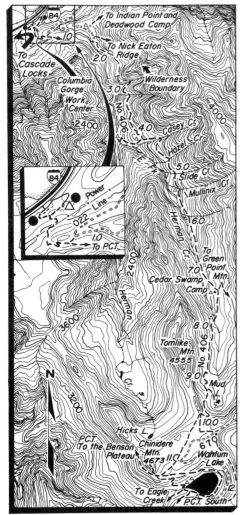

28 GREEN POINT MOUNTAIN– CASEY CREEK LOOP

One day trip or backpack
Distance: 19 miles round trip
Elevation gain: 4,750 feet; loss 100 feet
High point: 4,737 feet
Allow 10 to 11 hours round trip
Usually open June through November
Topographic maps:
  U.S.G.S. Carson, Wash.-Oreg.
  7.5'   1979
  U.S.G.S. Wahtum Lake, Oreg.
  7.5'   1979

Green Point Mountain is located at the infrequently visited south end of Nick Eaton Ridge and since the hike to it shares trailheads with three other interconnecting routes (No's. 27, 29 and 30), several loops are possible. Note that you may encounter horses on the part of the hike that follows the Herman Creek Trail.

From the west proceed on I-84 to the Cascade Locks Exit 44. Drive about 1.0 mile through the community to its east end and turn left where a sign marks the road to Industrial Park and Airport. After 2.0 miles cross over the freeway, turn left and in 0.4 mile come to the Columbia Gorge Work Center. Approaching from the east, take the Forest Lane–Herman Creek exit between the 48 and 47 mileposts. Go under the freeway, turn right and head west 0.6 mile to the Center. If the paved road to the campground is open, follow it up to trailhead parking. However, if it's blocked, turn right and drive to the northwest corner of the Work Center near the big green building. An obvious, though possibly unsigned, trail heads up from this alternate parking area and connects with the route from the campground.

Continue up from where the two trails join and cross a narrow power line access road. Traverse and after one set of short switchbacks come to the junction of the trail to the Benson Plateau (No. 26). Turn left and after 200 yards come to a large, flat open area. Cross it in the same direction you were heading and then keep right where you meet a dirt road. Climb along it, level off and pass the beginnings of the Gorton Creek and Nick Eaton Trails.

At 1.7 miles the road narrows into the Herman Creek Trail. Begin gradually dropping, pass two high waterfalls and then have a short section of uphill. Traverse into a large side canyon, pass the Columbia Wilderness boundary marker, ford Camp Creek and travel out the other side. Have a bit more downhill to another waterfall before beginning an easy climb along a less precipitous slope and at 4.1 miles come to the junction of the Casey Creek Trail No. 476 just before a campsite at a clearing. Taking this very steep route up to the Nick Eaton Trail and following the latter back makes an excellent shorter loop. After a level stretch on the main trail begin climbing steadily. Along the next two miles have easy crossings of three large streams and five smaller ones. At 7.3 miles come to the junction of the Herman Creek Cutoff No. 410 at dilapidated Cedar Swamp Shelter.

Turn left onto No. 410, walk on the level to a stream crossing, the last good source of water, and soon begin climbing. Pass through a swampy area and then continue switch backing uphill. At 9.3 miles level off and come to an old road, now officially designated as a trail. Head north from the road on the Gorton Creek Trail No. 408, which is level for 100 yards and then climbs to the summit of Green Point Mountain. After enjoying the extensive view, continue heading north near the edge of the open slope and then begin descending in woods.

Keep left at the junction of the Green Point Ridge Trail No. 418 and North Lake Trail No. 423 (refer to No. 31 for both) and after 1.5 miles of gradual downhill stay left again at the junction of the Plateau Cutoff Trail No. 412 to the Green Point Ridge Trail. Switch back down steeply, pass a sign stating Ridge Camp and a path heading east to water. Continue in more open terrain along the eastern side of the ridge to the junction of Nick Eaton Trail. Unless you intend to continue along the Gorton Creek Trail, which is the longest of the possible return routes, turn left onto Nick Eaton Trail. Climb briefly and then travel near the crest for 0.3 mile to the junction of the Casey Creek Trail. To follow it back, turn left and immediately begin the steep downhill. Pass a couple of open areas and also have several views over the upper end of the Herman Creek drainage and beyond to Mt. Hood.

Rainy Lake from Green Point Mountain

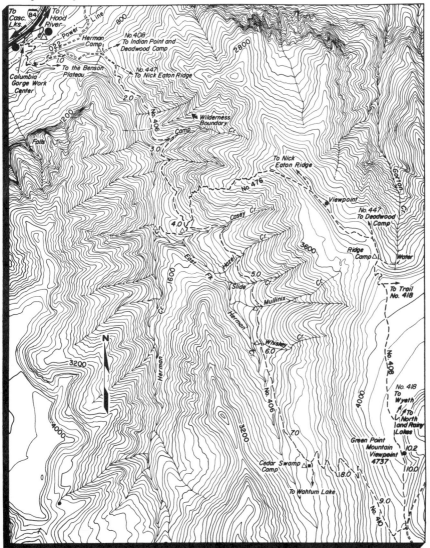

29 NICK EATON RIDGE

One day trip
Distance: 5.0 miles one way
Elevation gain: 4,100 feet; loss 100 feet
High point: 4,100 feet
Allow 3 to 3½ hours one way
Usually open late May through November
Topographic map:
U.S.G.S. Carson, Wash.-Oreg.
7.5'   1979

Of the four interconnecting trails that begin from the Columbia Gorge Work Center (No's. 27 through 30), this one offers the most far-ranging views. The two shortest of the several possible loops use either of the two connectors between the Gorton Creek and Nick Eaton Trails. Considerably more demanding combinations with the Nick Eaton Trail follow the Gorton Creek Trail to the crest of Nick Eaton Ridge or the Casey Creek Trail up from the Herman Creek Trail. To take full advantage of the views to the west, combine the routes so you return along the Nick Eaton Trail. Water is not available along the Nick Eaton Trail. You may encounter horses along the first 1.4 miles of the hike.

From the west proceed on I-84 to the Cascade Locks Exit 44. Drive about 1.0 mile through the community to its east end and turn left where a sign marks the road to Industrial Park and Airport. After 2.0 miles cross over the freeway, turn left and in 0.4 mile come to the Columbia Gorge Work Center. Approaching from the east, take the Forest Lane–Herman Creek exit between the 48 and 47 mileposts. Go under the freeway, turn right and head west 0.6 mile to the Center. If the paved road to the campground is open, follow it up to trailhead parking. However, if it's blocked, turn right and drive to the north-

west corner of the Work Center near the big green building. An obvious, though possibly unsigned, trail heads up from this alternate parking area and connects with the route from the campground.

Continue up from where the two trails join and cross a narrow power line access road. Traverse and after one set of short switchbacks come to the junction of the connector to the Pacific Crest Trail (No. 26). Turn left and after 200 yards come to a large, flat open area. Cross it in the same direction you were heading and then keep right where you meet a road. Climb along it, level off and at 1.4 miles pass the clearing at Herman Camp and the start of the Gorton Creek Trail. Follow the road 300 yards farther to the Nick Eaton Trail on your left. The road narrows into the Herman Creek Trail No. 277 after 250 yards.

Meander up through woods graced with much vine maple and then begin switch backing. Climb through two small open areas separated by woods populated with Oregon white oak to the third and largest clearing and corkscrew up it in six switchbacks. These meadows are smothered with wildflowers around mid May. Re-enter woods and wind up. Pass the sign marking the boundary of the Columbia Wilderness a short distance before coming to the junction at 3.4 miles of the 0.5 mile Ridge Cutoff Trail No. 437 to the Gorton Creek Trail.

Keep right (straight) and after several yards come to a large open slope where you'll have a good view of Mt. Hood and another look down the Columbia River. On a sunny day, this spot is an excellent place for a snack stop. Traverse into woods and descend in one switchback to a long saddle and the junction of the Deadwood Trail, which after 0.6 mile also connects with the Gorton Creek Trail. Cross the saddle, begin climbing and veer left onto the east side of the ridge. Traverse steeply up and farther on have views east to Wygant Peak (No. 35) and across the Columbia River to Dog (No. 3) and Wind Mountains and Mt. Adams. At 4.9 miles come to the crest, climb along more open terrain and have a view of Mt. Defiance (No. 33). A good stopping place is the area of rocky outcroppings at 5.1 miles just before the trail starts dropping. The Nick Eaton Trail passes the upper end of the Casey Creek Trail several hundred feet beyond this high point and continues along the crest 1.0 mile farther to its end at the junction with the Gorton Creek Trail. The latter heads south for another 2.0 miles to Green Point Mountain.

Aerial view — Nick Eaton Ridge and Mount Defiance

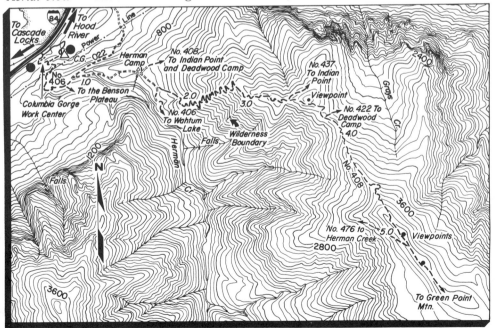

30 GORTON CREEK TRAIL

One day trip or backpack
Distance: 6.2 miles one way
Elevation gain: 4,200 feet; loss 200 feet
High point: 4,100 feet
Allow 4 hours one way
Usually open June through November
Topographic map:
U.S.G.S. Carson, Wash.-Oreg.
7.5′   1979

The Gorton Creek Trail shares the first 1.4 miles with hikes No's. 27, 28 and 29 and many return loops are possible along these interconnecting routes. Also, you can make a short side trip to Indian Point, a prominent rock pinnacle on the face of the Gorge. Later in the season, no water is available until 4.0 miles.

From the west proceed on I-84 to the Cascade Locks Exit 44. Drive about 1.0 mile through the community to its east end and turn left where a sign marks the road to Industrial Park and Airport. After 2.0 miles cross over the freeway, turn left and in 0.4 mile come to the Columbia Gorge Work Center. Approaching from the east, take the Forest Lane–Herman Creek exit between the 48 and 47 mileposts. Go under the freeway, turn right and head west 0.6 mile to the Center. If the paved road to the campground is open, follow it up to trailhead parking. However, if it's blocked, turn right and drive to the parking area at the northwest corner of the Work Center near the big green building. An obvious, though possibly unsigned, trail heads up from this alternate parking area and connects with the route from the campground.

Continue up from where the two trails join and cross a narrow power line access road. Traverse and after one set of short switchbacks come to the junction of the trail to the Benson Plateau (No. 26). Turn left and after 200 yards

come to a large, flat open area. Cross it in the same direction you were heading and then keep right on a dirt road. Climb along it, level off and at 1.4 miles turn left into the clearing at Herman Camp. After 300 yards the main road passes the start of the Nick Eaton Trail (No. 29) and 250 yards farther narrows into the Herman Creek Trail (No. 27).

The unsigned path between the start of the Gorton Creek Trail at the far end of Herman Camp and the outhouse on its north side is the final, although as of early 1988 uncompleted, section of the Gorge Trail No. 400 (see No. 31).

The Gorton Creek Trail starts as a faint old road but soon narrows to a single tread. Initially rise at a steep grade but soon wind up through the woods at a steady, moderate angle. Climb in three sets of switchbacks separated by traverses. Near 2.2 miles cross over the crest of a ridge, recross the nose in a switchback and make a long traverse to the south. Cross over three more ridge faces in the next 0.6 mile and come to the junction of the 0.5 mile long Ridge Cutoff Trail No. 437 to the Nick Eaton Trail.

Stay straight (left) and begin descending gradually. About 75 feet from the junction pass the unsigned use path that descends steeply for 0.2 mile to the base of Indian Point. The main trail continues dropping and a few yards beyond where it curves right and 0.8 mile from No. 437 come to the junction of the Deadwood Trail, which meets the Nick Eaton Trail in 0.6 mile. Keep left, cross Grays Creek and climb above Deadwood Camp.

The trail rises at a moderately steep grade in several short switchbacks to a view of Mt. Defiance (No. 33) and Dog Mountain (No. 3). Hike up along the crest, eventually at a steeper grade. Leave the ridge top and traverse gradually down along the east slope where you'll have more views. Continue mostly dropping, entering the Columbia Wilderness, and near the end of the descent cross a small stream, the last source of water. Resume climbing, make a set of switchbacks and continue steeply uphill. A level stretch offers a brief respite before the final climb to a junction on the crest. The route to the left goes to Green Point Mountain (No. 28).

Turn right, in 0.6 mile pass a rocky viewpoint and 0.2 mile farther come to the junction of Casey Creek Trail (No. 28). The Nick Eaton Trail continues north along the crest. In addition to surrounding you with different and excellent scenery, returning along either of these loops requires considerably less distance and uphill than retracing your steps.

Columbia River from Indian Point

31 WYETH TRAIL to NORTH LAKE

One day trip or backpack
Distance: 5.5 miles one way
Elevation gain: 4,100 feet; loss 100 feet
High point: 4,020 feet
Allow 4 hours one way
Usually open late May through November
Topographic map:
U.S.G.S. Carson, Wash.-Oreg.
7.5'   1979

Although the grade ranges from very steep to very, very steep between the 1.0 and 3.0 mile points, the climb from Wyeth to North Lake is popular with both hikers and backpackers. Views along the open sections include Mounts Adams, St. Helens and Defiance (No. 33), Wind and Dog (No. 3) Mountains and the fertile Carson Valley.

If reaching North Lake isn't demanding enough, you could continue another 1.1 miles to Rainy Lake just off Road 2820. Long loops involving car shuttles are possible by following less frequently used routes east from North Lake to Mt. Defiance or south from the junction at 4.2 miles to Green Point Mountain (No. 28).

Drive on I-84 to the Wyeth Exit 51. At the end of the exit turn right if you're coming from the west or, if you're approaching from the east, turn left and go under the freeway. Immediately come to a T-junction, turn right and after about 0.2 mile turn left into Wyeth Campground. If the road is blocked, park at the entrance. Whether driving or on foot, head south for 0.2 mile, staying straight (right) where loops head left, to trailhead parking at the road's end.

Walk along an old road bed for several hundred yards to the eastern terminus of the Gorge Trail No. 400. As of early 1988, only the eastern and westernmost portions of this final segment between Wyeth and Herman Camp (No. 30) had been completed. Turn left onto the Wyeth Trail, traverse and curve around to a north facing slope. The unsigned trail you pass on your left heads down to the campground and, if you parked at the entrance, following it back saves some distance. Walk through a cleared area under power lines, re-enter woods and ford a stream. Wind up through a forest where large, lacy, vine maples thrive between the widely spaced conifers. As you climb traverse the same rocky slope three times. From these open areas you can see down to the Columbia River and over a bucolic scene along Herman Creek Road.

Continue steeply up to the edge of the canyon holding Harphan Creek. The pinnacle jutting up from the north face of the ridge to the west is Indian Point (No. 30). Keep climbing but farther on have a brief lessening of the grade and even a wee bit of downhill. Come to the edge of the canyon a second time and resume rising very steeply to a stream crossing at 2.5 miles. Continue up beside the creek along the steepest grade of the hike, again come to the canyon's edge and begin traveling along a narrow, rocky crest. Wind up over an open area that, not surprisingly, affords fine views to the north. As you've no doubt figured out by here, the vivid pink streamers several tenths mile below and above the stream crossing mark a more moderate alignment. However, the people in charge of trails subsequently decided to reevaluate the entire Wyeth Trail, not just the very steepest portions, before starting any rebuilding.

Travel up in woods, skirting the western edge of a large swath of talus, pass a brushy area and then cross one last open patch before re-entering woods. Climb in eight long switchbacks, passing the boundary marker for the Columbia Wilderness along one of them, and then walk at a gradual grade to the junction of the Green Point Ridge Trail No. 418 at 4.2 miles.

Stay left, soon begin traversing downhill and have views of Mt. Defiance. Come to a small level area that is swampy early in the season, continue downhill a bit farther and cross a stream. Resume climbing, passing a brushy clearing on your left and farther on hopping two small streams, to a signed junction. Turn sharply right and walk 30 yards to the earth dam at North Lake.

To reach Rainy Lake or Mt. Defiance, continue south from the junction just before the lake for 75 yards to a fork and turn right to reach the former or left for the latter.

Fisherman at North Lake

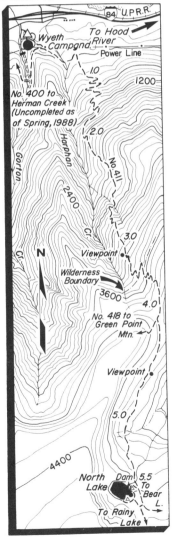

32 SHELLROCK MOUNTAIN

One-half day trip
Distance: 1.3 miles one way
Elevation gain: 1,200 feet
High point: 1,300 feet
Allow 1 hour one way
Usually open February through December
Topographic map:
  U.S.G.S. Mt. Defiance, Oreg.-Wash.
  7.5′   **1979**

Among the characteristic features encountered on many hikes on the Oregon side of the Gorge are the swaths of moss covered talus that sprawl against sections of the tread. People who are captivated by these proto-rock gardens will especially enjoy the short hike up Shellrock Mountain, across the Columbia River from cone shaped Wind Mountain, because three-quarters of the trip is on such a slope. Be assured that there is a trail and that no boulder hopping is involved. However, because the tread has been built on rocks, your feet will be much happier wearing boots than athletic shoes.

Three very short side trips, one to a grassy viewpoint and two along an interesting old road, are added attractions. People who want more hiking for their driving time can create a perfect duo by combining the Shellrock Mountain trip

with the 2.0 mile loop along the lower part of the Starvation Ridge Trail (No. 34). No water sources are available on Shellrock Mountain.

From the west proceed on I-84 about 0.8 mile east of the 52 milepost to just beyond the east end of a high, steel retaining wall above the freeway and park at a faint segment of the original Columbia River Highway where a small, white sign states *Property of Oregon Department of Transportation*. This retaining wall is in three sections and there're a hundred feet or so between its most easterly end and the parking space. Beyond the turnout you can see a sign off the freeway shoulder warning of *Rocks* and behind that another one stating *Rest Area 2 Miles*. To return westbound after the hike you'll have to drive east 3.0 miles to the Viento Park Interchange. If you're approaching from the east, go to the Wyeth Interchange near the 51 milepost and then head east about 1.6 miles to the trailhead.

Walk east along the old roadbed for 75 yards and then turn onto a obscure, rocky path that heads up from the right shoulder. After several feet curve left and traverse up to the east along an obvious tread. Climb more steeply in six short switchbacks to an old wagon road. The section to the west unfortunately ends in a rockslide after several hundred yards but it's still fun to follow that far.

Turn left and walk east along the old road about 75 yards to the edge of the woods where the trail resumes winding up the rocky slope. The section of the road that continues east also abruptly stops in several hundred yards but this time the truncation was caused by severe stream erosion.

Where the main trail makes its second turn on the rock swath a side path heads east to a steep, grassy perch below power lines. Switch back nine more times along the main trail, enjoying increasingly good views to the east as you gain elevation.

Enter sparse woods and switch back four times, mostly along a northeast facing slope. Make a long traverse to the south, switch back a final time and then travel north and west to a clearing. The small structure several yards downslope is an observation station built by the U.S. Geological Survey for monitoring possible land slippage in the Wind Mountain area.

The summit of Shellrock Mountain is 800 feet above the clearing. Apparently, a trail never was constructed beyond 1.4 miles and reaching the top cross-country involves considerable bushwhacking.

Old roadbed on Shellrock Mountain

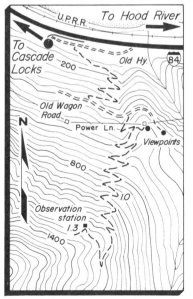

33 MT. DEFIANCE

One day trip
Distance: 6 miles one way
Elevation gain: 4,815 feet
High point: 4,960 feet
Allow 4 to 5 hours one way
Usually open June through October
Topographic map:
U.S.G.S. Mt. Defiance, Oreg.-Wash.
7.5'   1979

Although Mt. Defiance is the highest point in the Gorge and a popular conditioning hike for mountaineers, the trail to its summit is not the hardest because the route never has long stretches of extremely steep tread and there are several sections of moderate grades. Hikers who do enjoy unremitting, muscle stretching uphill can make a loop by taking the Starvation Ridge Trail (No. 34) up and returning along the Mt. Defiance Trail.

Far-ranging views to the north, east and west are enjoyed along much of the Mt. Defiance Trail and the panorama from the summit includes the major peaks from Mt. Rainier south to Mt. Hood, a bird's-eye view down onto the Upper and Lower Hood River Valleys and beyond to the wheat fields of eastern Oregon.

From the west drive on I-84 about 55 miles from Portland to the Starvation Creek Rest Area parking lot. To return west bound after the hike head east 0.8 mile to the Viento Park interchange. If you're approaching from the east, travel on I-84 to the Wyeth exit near milepost 51 and then drive east 4.0 miles.

Walk west back along the entrance road to a sign stating *Mt. Defiance Trail*. Parallel the freeway on the south side of a concrete barricade to a section of the original Columbia River Highway and pass the signed lower end of Trail 414B, a cutoff to the Starvation Ridge Trail. Stay straight on the old road, pass Cabin Creek Falls and begin traveling through woods on a trail. Curve sharply left into a clearing, ford Warren Creek below Hole-in-the-Wall Falls and traverse up for 0.2 mile to the signed junction of the

Starvation Ridge Trail No. 414.

Stay straight (right), continue traversing and pass Lancaster Falls, the last easily accessible and plentiful source of water. A bit farther follow a power line cut and then begin a series of short switchbacks. Travel along the east facing slope of a side canyon to a sign identifying the 150 foot spur to the final source of water. Climb more steeply in short switchbacks to the edge of Lindsey Creek canyon. Walk on the level for several yards across a faint old logging road and then traverse a slope of grass, trees and, in spring, wildflowers, before again switch backing. Pass a second viewpoint on the canyon's edge and continue winding up the face of the ridge to its crest at 2.8 miles. Enjoy 0.2 mile of level grade before resuming the uphill, initially on an old road bed and then along a trail.

Around 4.0 miles begin climbing through an area of smaller conifers near a ridge crest. Leave the woods and wind up an open area near the edge of a steep, rocky slope and then traverse to a level boulder field. Except while you're on the summit of Mt. Defiance, which is just outside the preserve, you'll be in the Columbia Wilderness for the remainder of the hike. Resume climbing moderately and come to the junction of the sometimes faint Mitchell Point Trail No. 417 that descends for 0.7 mile to Warren Lake, 550 feet below.

Turn right and continue up for 0.1 mile to a switchback to the right. The faint tread that continues straight is the original alignment and the route of a possible return loop from the summit. Turn right and traverse gradually uphill along the open slope where you'll have fine views, many of which can't be seen from the summit. Curve south, travel briefly up through woods and then make a long traverse on a talus slope. Below is Bear Lake and Green Point Mountain (No. 28) is the high point on the ridge beyond. Have a fine view of Mt. Hood and come to the junction of Trail No. 413 that descends past the spur to Bear Lake and reaches Road 2820 in 1.4 miles.

Turn left, make three short switchbacks and head north to the summit where a microwave installation occupies the site once graced by a tall, wooden fire lookout. To make that shorter return loop, walk to the northeast corner of the building and look for a large, old reddish-brown sign on a tree stating *Mt. Defiance Trail*. Follow the well defined path down to Road 2821, cross it and continue descending. Where you come to 2821 a second time veer right a few yards to pick up the tread.

Hiker at Lancaster Falls

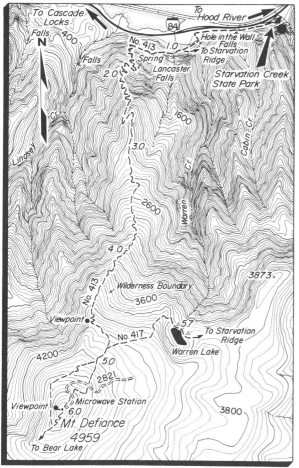

34 STARVATION RIDGE TRAIL to WARREN LAKE

One day trip or backpack
Distance: 6 miles one way
Elevation gain: 4,050 feet; loss 350 feet
High point: 3,850 feet
Allow 3½ to 4 hours one way
Usually open June through October
Topographic map:
  U.S.G.S. Mt. Defiance, Oreg.-Wash.
  7.5'   1979

Hikers who feel like a short, rigorous workout instead of the long, demanding one to Warren Lake can make a delightful loop by following the lower end of the Starvation Ridge Trail to the highest and last of the grassy, open crests at 2.2 miles and then returning by a short connector to the starting point. This beginning section of the hike is especially attractive around mid April when a profusion of wildflowers puts on one of the best shows in the Gorge. Energetic types who relish long, strenuous workouts will savor the opportunity to continue from Warren Lake up along an initially faint route to Mt. Defiance and then return along the Mt. Defiance Trail (No. 33). People who have the strength and endurance to reach Warren Lake shouldn't have any trouble with the extra 1,200 feet of uphill and 2.0 miles this circuit involves. However, they can halve that extra distance and climbing by skipping the leg to the summit and returning directly down the Mt. Defiance Trail No. 413.

From the west proceed on I-84 about 55 miles from Portland to the Starvation Creek Rest Area parking lot. To return westbound after the hike you'll have to head east 0.8 mile to the Viento Park interchange. If you're approaching from the east, travel on I-84 to the Wyeth exit near milepost 51 and then drive east 4.0 miles to the Starvation Creek Rest Area.

Walk west back along the entrance road to the rest area to a sign stating *Mt. Defiance Trail*. Parallel the freeway on the south side of a concrete barricade to a section of the original Columbia River Highway and pass the signed lower end of Trail No. 414B, a 0.5 mile connector to the Starvation Ridge Trail and the return route of the short loop. Stay straight on the old roadbed, pass Cabin Creek Falls and begin traveling on a trail proper through woods. Curve sharply left into a clearing, ford Warren Creek below Hole-in-the-Wall Falls and traverse up for 0.2 mile to the signed junction of the Starvation Ridge Trail.

Turn left, traverse along the steep slope and curve into the side canyon holding Warren Creek. Ford it and after one set of switchbacks come to the first of the open, grassy slopes. After half a dozen more turns come to a crest where you can look ahead down onto a viewpoint. Descend past the unsigned short path to the overlook and continue winding down in woods to the ford of Cabin Creek, the last easily accessible source of water. Several hundred feet up from the crossing come to the signed junction of the upper end of the Starvation Cutoff Trail No. 414B.

Stay right and climb to an area of oaks and grass. Wind up in a total of 14 moderately steep switchbacks of varying lengths, with some in woods and others along open slopes, to a crest at a power line tower, the suggested turnaround point for people making the short loop. Here's a fine spot to leisurely study the barge traffic on the river, the trains and vehicles snaking along both banks and scenic landmarks, such as Dog Mountain (No. 3) directly across the river.

Turn right at the crest, enter woods and climb mostly along the ridge top at a generally steep grade. At 3.7 miles keep left at a possibly unsigned path that goes to water. Near 4.1 miles cross a small scree slope and then re-enter woods and begin a series of short switchbacks. Traverse a larger scree area on a wide trail and have another stretch in woods before coming to an old logging road. Follow the bed for a few hundred feet to the resumption of the trail on the right. Climb in four switchbacks and at 5.0 miles travel above a newer logging road and clearcut. Hike uphill, level off on a crest and pass a viewpoint. Continue on the level through open and then wooded terrain to the junction of a route that goes 150 feet south to Road 630. Turn right and descend gradually for 0.4 mile to Warren Lake, which is in the easternmost portion of the Columbia Wilderness.

To make the possible loop, head west from the junction 50 yards above the lake, walk around the north shore and then wind up in a generally westerly direction along a sometimes obscure tread to the Mt. Defiance Trail.

Warren Lake

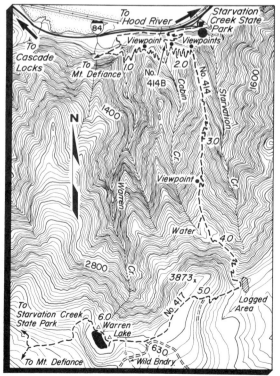

35 WYGANT TRAIL

One day trip
**Distance: 3.8 miles one way to Wygant
Peak**
Elevation gain: 2,200 feet; loss 100 feet
High point: 2,214 feet
Allow 2 to 2½ hours one way
Usually open March through November
Topographic maps:
   U.S.G.S. Hood River, Oreg.-Wash.
   7.5'   1979
   U.S.G.S. Mt. Defiance, Oreg.-Wash.
   7.5'   1979

The circuitous Wygant Trail offers a mix of varied scenery including grassy slopes with gnarled Oregon white oaks, evergreen woods the equal of those encountered farther west in the more moist sections of the Gorge, several rocky viewpoints affording especially good views to the east and a section along the original Columbia River Highway. Thanks to the volunteer trail building of Portlander Basil Clark and friends, a loop is now possible between the 0.9 and 2.7 mile points.

From the west drive on I-84 for 0.4 mile beyond the 58 mile post to an unsigned exit. At the end of the exit turn right and then left, following the sign to parking at Lausmann Park picnic area where there are toilet facilities. The imposing rock mass directly overhead is Mitchell Point. To return west bound after the hike, continue east on I-84 another 3.4 miles to Exit 62. Approaching from the east, proceed on I-84 to the Viento Park exit near the 56 mile post and then travel east 2.5 miles to the unsigned exit.

Walk back to the junction where you turned left but keep straight and continue west along a road. Just before the pavement ends look left for some of the vegetation covered foundations that mark the former community of Sonny. During the first 15 years of the 1900's, this settlement contained a family home plus the buildings and paraphernalia that serviced the lumber operation here. Continue west along the

dirt road for 100 feet or so, where it curves sharply up to the left stay straight and after several yards begin traveling on a trail. Cross a stream in a little side canyon and then descend to another section of the old highway. Walk along the road for about 0.3 mile to side canyon on your left whose stream has washed away the moss. Turn left, walk several yards along the east side of the canyon floor to the resumption of the trail, cross to the opposite wall and wind up in four switchbacks. Travel at a more gradual grade along a bench and 100 feet before you meet the edge of Perham Creek canyon come to the lower end of the Chetwoot Trail, the route of the recommended return loop.

From the junction at the edge of Perham Creek canyon the spur to the right goes to a viewpoint and the main trail heads left down the oak covered wall to a bridge, which like most wooden spans can be slippery when wet. Traverse uphill to an open, grassy viewpoint. The trail almost doubles back from the overlook and after a few hundred feet crosses an old road. Switch back and travel east along the cleared swath under power lines and then curve right into a wooded side canyon. Climb in a series of short traverses and switchbacks, passing viewpoints in settings of grass and oaks at two of the turns.

Make a long, gradual traverse, switch back and at the end of another traverse come to the signed junction of the upper end of the Chetwoot Trail. To continue to Wygant Peak, make the switchback to the right, eventually curve into a side canyon and make three turns to yet another viewpoint. For the next mile climb in 15 switchbacks at a steady grade through woods and near the ridge crest. Occasionally, the trail changes from the east to the west sides or passes through grassy clearings with views of Wind and Dog (No. 3) Mountains. Walk along the crest of an east-west oriented ridge and then make two short switchbacks to the small clearing that marks the end of the hike.

The tread of the Chetwoot Trail is more rustic than the Wygant Trail but that's part of the former's charm. As you might have guessed from Mr. Clark's whimsical painted wooden signs, chetwoot is an Indian word for bear and an encounter with one, not as timid as they usually are, inspired the name. From the upper end of the Chetwoot Trail at 2.7 miles contour along a steep, open slope and then travel in and out of the canyon holding Perham Creek. Where you come to the power line cut, look right for one of those droll signs marking the resumption of the trail.

Bridge over Perham Creek

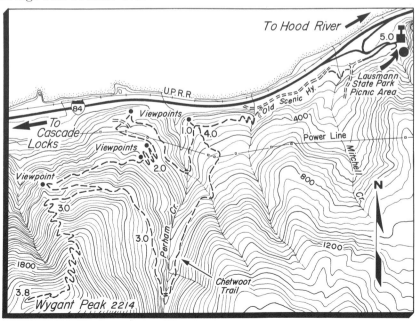

ALPHABETICAL INDEX OF TRAILS

Cover photos: Multnomah Falls
Starvation Ridge Trail
Oneonta Trail